grzimek's
Student Animal Life Resource

• • • •

grzimek's
Student Animal Life Resource

• • • •

Amphibians
volume 2

Leptodactylid frogs to Shovel-nosed frogs

Leslie A. Mertz, PhD, and
Catherine Judge Allen, MA, ELS, authors

Madeline S. Harris, project editor
Neil Schlager and Jayne Weisblatt, editors

THOMSON

GALE

Detroit • New York • San Francisco • San Diego • New Haven, Conn. • Waterville, Maine • London • Munich

Grzimek's Student Animal Life Resource: Amphibians

Leslie A. Mertz, PhD, and Catherine Judge Allen, MA, ELS

Project Editor
Madeline S. Harris

Editorial
Stephanie Cook, Heather Price,
Lemma Shomali

Indexing Services
Synapse, the Knowledge Link
Corporation

Rights and Acquisitions
Margaret Abendroth, Timothy Sisler

Imaging and Multimedia
Randy Bassett, Michael Logusz, Dan
Newell, Chris O'Bryan, Robyn Young

Product Design
Tracey Rowens, Jennifer Wahi

Composition
Evi Seoud, Mary Beth Trimper

Manufacturing
Wendy Blurton, Dorothy Maki

LIBRARY OF CONGRESS CATALOGING-IN-PUBLICATION DATA

Mertz, Leslie A.
Grzimek's student animal life resource. Amphibians / Leslie A. Mertz and Catherine Judge Allen, authors; Neil Schlager and Jayne Weisblatt, editors.
   p. cm.
   Includes bibliographical references and index.
   ISBN 0-7876-9407-X (set hardcover : alk. paper) — ISBN 0-7876-9408-8 (volume 1) — ISBN 0-7876-9409-6 (volume 2) — ISBN 0-7876-9410-X (volume 3)
   1. Amphibians—Juvenile literature. I. Allen, Catherine Judge. II. Schlager, Neil, 1966– III. Weisblatt, Jayne. IV. Title.
   QL644.2.M4263 2005
   597.8—dc22   2005015192

This title is also available as an e-book
Contact your Thomson Gale sales representative for ordering information.

Printed in Canada
10 9 8 7 6 5 4 3 2 1

Contents

Reader's Guide

Grzimek's Student Animal Life Resource: Amphibians offers readers comprehensive and easy-to-use information on Earth's amphibians. Order entries provide an overview of a group of families, and family entries provide an overview of a particular family. Entries are arranged by taxonomy, the science through which living things are classified into related groups. Each entry includes sections on physical characteristics; geographic range; habitat; diet; behavior and reproduction; animals and people; and conservation status. All entries are followed by one or more species accounts with the same information as well as a range map and photo or illustration for each species. Entries conclude with a list of books, periodicals, and Web sites that may be used for further research.

ADDITIONAL FEATURES

Each volume of *Grzimek's Student Animal Life Resource: Amphibians* includes a pronunciation guide for scientific names, a glossary, an overview of amphibians, a list of species in the set by biome, a list of species by geographic location, and an index. The set has 221 full-color maps, photos, and illustrations to enliven the text, and sidebars provide additional facts and related information.

NOTE

Grzimek's Student Animal Life Resource: Amphibians has standardized information in the Conservation Status section. The IUCN Red List provides the world's most comprehensive inventory of the global conservation status of plants and animals. Using a set of criteria to evaluate extinction risk, the IUCN recognizes the following categories: Extinct, Extinct in the Wild, Critically Endangered, Endangered, Vulnerable, Conservation Dependent, Near Threatened, Least Concern, and Data Deficient. These terms are defined where they are used in the text, but for a complete explanation of each category, visit the IUCN web page at http://www.iucn.org/themes/ssc/redlists/RL cats2001booklet.html.

ACKNOWLEDGEMENTS

Gale would like to thank several individuals for their assistance with this set. Leslie Mertz and Catherine Judge Allen wrote the text for the volumes. At Schlager Group Inc., Jayne Weisblatt and Neil Schlager coordinated the writing and editing of the set.

Special thanks are also due for the invaluable comments and suggestions provided by the *Grzimek's Student Animal Life Resource: Amphibians* advisors:

- Mary Alice Anderson, Media Specialist, Winona Middle School, Winona, Minnesota
- Thane Johnson, Librarian, Oklahoma City Zoo, Oklahoma City, Oklahoma
- Debra Kachel, Media Specialist, Ephrata Senior High School, Ephrata, Pennsylvania
- Nina Levine, Media Specialist, Blue Mountain Middle School, Courtlandt Manor, New York
- Ruth Mormon, Media Specialist, The Meadows School, Las Vegas, Nevada

COMMENTS AND SUGGESTIONS

We welcome your comments on *Grzimek's Student Animal Life Resource: Amphibians* and suggestions for future editions of this work. Please write: Editors, *Grzimek's Student Animal Life Resource: Amphibians*, U•X•L, 27500 Drake Rd., Farmington Hills, Michigan 48331-3535; call toll free: 1-800-877-4253; fax: 248-699-8097; or send e-mail via www.gale.com.

Pronunciation Guide for Scientific Names

Acanthixalus spinosus ay-kan-THICK-sal-us spy-NO-sus

Adelotus brevis ay-deh-LO-tus BREH-vis

Adenomus kandianus ay-deh-NO-mus kan-die-AY-nus

Albericus siegfriedi al-BEAR-ih-kus SIG-freed-eye

Alexteroon jynx ay-LEKS-tih-roh-on jinks

Allophryne ruthveni ah-lo-FRYN rooth-VEN-eye

Allophrynidae ah-lo-FRY-nih-dee

Alytes obstetricans ah-LYE-tes ob-STET-trih-kanz

Ambystoma tigrinum am-bih-STOH-ma tih-GRIH-num

Ambystomatidae am-bih-stoh-MA-tih-dee

Amphiuma tridactylum am-fee-U-ma try-DAK-tih-lum

Amphiumidae am-fee-U-mih-dee

Aneides lugubris ay-NEE-ih-deez lu-GU-bris

Ansonia longidigita an-SOH-nee-aye lon-jih-DIJ-ih-ta

Anura ann-UR-uh

Arenophryne rotunda ah-ree-no-FRYN roh-TUN-da

Arthroleptidae ar-throh-LEP-tih-dee

Arthroleptis stenodactylus ar-throh-LEP-tis sten-oh-DAK-tih-lus

Ascaphidae as-KAF-ih-dee

Ascaphus montanus as-KAF-us mon-TAN-us

Assa darlingtoni AY-suh dar-ling-TON-eye

Atelognathus patagonicus ay-teh-log-NAYTH-us pat-ah-GO-nih-kus

Atelopus varius ay-teh-LO-pus var-ee-us

Atelopus vogli ay-teh-LO-pus vohg-lye

Barbourula busuangensis bar-bo-RU-la bus-u-an-JEN-sis

Bolitoglossa pesrubra bo-LYE-toh-glos-sah pes-ROO-bra

Bombina bombina BOM-bin-ah BOM-bin-ah

Bombina orientalis BOM-bin-ah oh-ree-en-TAL-ihs

Bombina variegata BOM-bin-ah vay-ree-GA-ta

Bombinatoridae BOM-bin-ah-TOR-ih-dee

Brachycephalidae brak-ee-sef-FAL-ih-dee

Brachycephalus ephippium brak-ee-SEF-fal-us ee-FIP-ee-um

Brachycephalus nodoterga brak-ee SEF-fal-us no-DOE-tur-ga

Brachycephalus pernix brak-ee-SEF-fal-us PER-nicks

Brachycephalus vertebralis brak-ee-SEF-fal-us ver-teh-BRA-lis

Brachytarsophrys intermedia brak-ee-TAR-so-frys in-tur-ME-dee-uh

Bufo marinus BOO-foe MAYR-ih-nus

Bufo periglenes BOO-foe pair-ee-GLEH-nees

Bufonidae boo-FOH-nih-dee

Bymnophiona bim-no-fee-OH-nuh

Caecilian seh-SILL-ee-uhn

Caeciliidae seh-SILL-ee-eye-dee

Caudata kaw-DAY-tuh

Centrolene geckoideum SEN-troh-lean gek-oh-EYE-dee-um

Centrolenidae sen-troh-LEN-ih-dee

Ceratophrys cornuta seh-RAT-oh-fris kor-NEW-ta

Chioglossa lusitanica chee-oh-GLOSS-ah loo-sih-TAN-ih-ka

Cochranella ignota kok-ran-ELL-ah ihg-NO-ta

Cochranella saxiscandens kok-ran-ELL-ah saks-ee-SKAN-denz

Colostethus caeruleodactylus coh-loh-STETH-us see-RUE-lee-oh-DAK-til-us

Conraua goliath kon-RAH-u-ah go-LYE-eth

Cophixalus riparius co-FIX-ah-lus rih-PAIR-ee-us

Cryptobranchidae KRIP-toe-BRAN-kih-dee

Cryptobranchus alleganiensis krip-toe-BRAN-cus al-lee-GAY-nee-en-sis

Cyclorana platycephala sy-klo-RA-na plat-ee-SEF-fa-la

Cynops pyrrhogaster sy-NOPS pie-roh-GAS-ter

Dendrobatidae den-droh-BA-tih-dee

Dermophis mexicanus der-MO-fis meks-ih-KAN-us

Desmognathus fuscus dez-mog-NATH-us FUS-cus

Dicamptodon tenebrosus di-CAMP-toe-don ten-eh-BROH-sus

Dicamptodontidae di-CAMP-toe-DON-tih-dee

Discoglossidae dis-ko-GLOSS-ih-dee

Discoglossus pictus dis-ko-GLOSS-us PIK-tus

Edalorhina perezi ed-dah-LOR-heena PER-ez-eye

Epicrionops marmoratus eh-pee-KREE-oh-nops mar-moh-RA-
tus

Epipedobates tricolor eh-pee-ped-oh-BA-tees tri-KUL-or

Eurycea bislineata u-REE-see-uh bis-LIN-ee-ah-ta

Eurycea rathbuni u-REE-see-uh rath-BUN-eye

Gastrophryne carolinensis GAS-troh-fryn kay-roh-LIN-en-sis

Gastrotheca riobambae gas-troh-THEH-ka ree-oh-BAM-bee

Gymnophiona jim-no-fee-OH-nuh

Heleophryne natalensis heh-lee-oh-FRYN nay-TAL-en-sis

Heleophrynidae heh-lee-oh-FRYN-ih-dee

Hemiphractus proboscideus heh-mee-FRAK-tus proh-BOSS-
kid-day-us

Hemisotidae heh-mee-SAW-tih-dee

Hemisus barotseensis heh-MEE-sus bare-aht-SEEN-sis

Hemisus marmatorus heh-MEE-sus mar-mah-TOR-us

Hemisus sudanensis heh-MEE-sus soo-dan-EN-sis

Hyalinobatrachium valerioi high-ah-LIN-oh-bah-TRAK-ee-um
vah-LAIR-ree-oh-eye

Hyla leucophyllata HIGH-lah loo-ko-fye-LAT-ta

Hylidae HIGH-lih-dee

Hynobiidae high-no-BEE-eye-dee

Hynobius retardatus high-NO-bee-us ree-tar-DAT-tus

Hyperoliidae high-per-OLE-lee-eye-dee

Hyperolius marginatus high-per-OLE-lee-us mar-jin-AT-tus

Hyperolius marmoratus high-per-OLE-lee-us mar-more-AT-tus

Hyperolius viridiflavus high-per-OLE-lee-us vir-rid-ih-FLA-vus

Ichthyophiidae ik-thee-oh-FYE-eye-dee

Ichthyophis glutinosus ik-thee-OH-fis gloo-tin-OH-sus

Kaloula pulchra kah-LOW-oo-la PULL-kra

Kassina senegalensis kah-see-na sen-ee-gall-EN-sis

Leiopelma hamiltoni lay-oh-PEL-ma ham-il-TO-nye

Leiopelma pakeka lay-oh-PEL-ma pa-KEY-ka

Leiopelmatidae lay-oh-pel-MAH-tih-dee

Lepidobatrachus laevis lep-ee-doh-bah-TRAK-us lay-EH-vis

Leptobrachium banae lep-toh-BRAK-ee-um BAN-nee

Leptodactylidae lep-toh-dak-TIL-ih-dee

Leptodactylus pentadactylus lep-toh-dak-TIL-us pen-ta-DAK-
til-us

Limnodynastidae lim-no-dye-NAS-tih-dee
Lithodytes lineatus lih-thoh-DYE-teez lin-ee-AT-tus
Litoria caerulea lih-TOR-ree-uh seh-RU-lee-uh
Mantidactylus liber man-ti-DAK-til-us LEE-ber
Megophryidae me-go-FRY-ih-dee
Megophrys montana me-go-FRIS mon-TAN-ah
Micrixalus phyllophilus my-krik-SAL-us fye-LO-fil-us
Microbatrachella capensis my-kro-bah-trak-ELL-la cap-PEN-sis
Microhyla karunaratnei my-kro-HIGH-la kare-roo-nah-RAT-nee-eye
Microhylidae my-kro-HIGH-lih-dee
Myobatrachidae my-oh-bat-TRAK-ih-dee
Nasikabatrachidae nas-SIK-ka-bat-TRAK-ih-dee
Nasikabatrachus sahyadrensis nas-SIK-ka-bat-TRAK-us sa-HIGH-ah-dren-sis
Necturus maculosus nek-TOO-rus mak-u-LOH-sus
Neobatrachus pictus nee-oh-bat-TRAK-us PIK-tus
Notaden melanoscaphus NO-tah-den mel-an-oh-SKAF-us
Nyctixalus pictus nik-TIK-sal-us PIK-tus
Occidozyga lima ock-sih-DOZE-ih-gah LEE-ma
Onychodactylus japonicus on-ik-oh-DAK-til-us ja-PON-ih-kus
Oreolalax schmidti oh-ree-oh-LA-laks SCHMIDT-eye
Otophryne pyburni oh-toe-FRYN pie-BURN-eye
Parhoplophryne usambarica par-HOP low-fryn u-sam-BAR-ee-ka
Pelobatidae pel-low-BA-tih-dee
Pelodytes punctatus pel-low-DYE-teez punk-TAH-tus
Philautus papillosus fil-LAW-tus pa-pill-OH-sus
Philoria pughi fil-LOW-ree-uh PYU-eye
Phrynomantis bifasciatus fry-no-MAN-tis bi-FAS-see-at-tus
Phyllobates terribilis fye-low-BA-teez ter-rib-BIL-iss
Pipa pipa PIE-pa PIE-pa
Pipidae PIE-pih-dee
Plethodontidae pleth-oh-DON-tih-dee
Pleurodema bufonina PLOOR-oh-dee-ma boo-fo-NEE-na
Proteidae pro-TEE-ih-dee
Proteus anguinus PRO-tee-us AN-gwin-us
Pseudis paradoxa SOO-dis pair-ah-DOKS-sa
Pseudoeurycea bellii soo-doe-yur-EE-see-ah BELL-ee-eye
Rachophorus arboreus rak-OH-for-us ar-bor-EE-us
Rana catesbeiana RAH-nah kat-TEEZ-bee-eye-an-uh

Rana temporaria RAH-nah tem-po-RARE-ee-uh

Ranidae RAH-nee-dee

Ranodon sibiricus RAH-no-don sib-EAR-ee-kus

Rhacophoridae rak-oh-FOR-ih-dee

Rhinatrematidae rye-na-tree-MA-tih-dee

Rhinoderma darwinii rye-no-DER-ma dar-WIN-ee-eye

Rhinodermatidae rye-no-der-MA-tih-dee

Rhinophrynidae rye-no-FRY-nih-dee

Rhinophrynus dorsalis rye-no-FRY-nus DOR-suh-lis

Rhyacotriton cascadae rye-YA-koh-try-ton KAS-kah-dee

Rhyacotritonidae rye-ya-koh-try-TON-nih-dee

Salamandra salamandra sal-a-MAN-dra sal-a-MAN-dra

Salamandridae sal-a-MAN-drih-dee

Scaphiophryne calcarata skaf-FEE-oh-fryn kal-ka-RAT-ta

Scaphiophryne gottlebei skaf-FEE-oh-fryn got-LEB-ee-eye

Scaphiophrynidae skaf-fee-oh-FRYN-nih-dee

Scarthyla goinorum skar-THIGH-la go-in-OR-um

Scolecomorphidae skoh-lee-kom-MOR-fih-dee

Scolecomorphus kirkii skoh-lee-kom-MOR-fus KIRK-ee-eye

Silurana tropicalis sil-u-RA-na trop-ih-KAL-is

Siren intermedia SIGH-ren in-ter-ME-dee-uh

Sirenidae sigh-REN-nih-dee

Sooglossidae soo-GLOSS-sih-dee

Sooglossus sechellensis soo-GLOSS-sus say-shell-EN-sis

Stumpffia helenae STUM-fee-uh hell-LEN-ah-ee

Taudactylus eungellensis taw-DAK-til-us ee-u-jel-LEN-sis

Thoropa miliaris thor-OH-pa mil-ee-AIR-iss

Trichobatrachus robustus try-koh-ba-TRAK-us roh-BUS-tus

Triprion petasatus TRIP-pree-on pet-TAS-sah-tus

Triturus cristatus TRY-ter-us krih-STAT-us

Triturus vulgaris TRY-ter-us vul-GARE-iss

Tylototriton verrucosus tie-LOW-tow-try-tun ver-ruh-KOH-sus

Typhlonectes compressicauda tie-flo-NEK-teez kom-press-sih-KAW-duh

Uraeotyphlus oxyurus u-ray-ee-oh-TIE-flus oks-ee-YUR-us

Uraeotyphylidae u-ray-ee-oh-tie-FIE-lih-dee

Vibrissaphora ailaonica vie-brih-saf-FOR-uh ale-la-ON-nik-ah

Xenopus laevis zee-NA-pus lay-EH-vis

Words to Know

A

Adaptable organism An organism that can adjust to various living conditions.

Ambush A style of hunting in which a predator hides and waits for an unsuspecting prey animal to come to it.

Amphibian A vertebrate that has moist, smooth skin; is cold-blooded, meaning the body temperature is the same as the temperature of the surroundings; and, in most instances, has a two-stage life cycle.

Amplexus In frogs, a mating position in which the male clings to the female's back.

Amphipods Beach fleas, water lice, and other small water-living invertebrates.

Aposematic coloration Warning colors that advertise something about an animal, possibly its bad-tasting, poisonous skin.

Aquatic Living in the water.

Arboreal Living in trees.

Arthropods Insects, spiders, and other invertebrates that have jointed legs.

B

Balancers Structures on the sides of the head of some salamander larvae that support the head until the legs develop.

Barbels Little bits of flesh sometimes seen dangling from the mouth or chin of animals, such as some frogs and fishes.

Bask Sunbathe; often seen in reptiles and amphibians to help warm up their bodies.

Bioindicator species An organism that people can use to tell whether or not the environment is healthy.

Bromeliads Plants of warm, usually tropical, forests that often grow on other plants. Their leaves typically overlap into cup shapes that can hold water.

C

Cannibalistic Describing animals that eat other members of their own species.

Carnivorous Meat-eating.

Cartilage A flexible material in an animal's body that is often associated with bones.

Chorus In male frogs, a group that calls together.

Chromosomes The structures in a cell that hold the DNA.

Cloaca The chamber in some animals that holds waste from the kidneys and intestines, holds eggs or sperm about to be released to the outside, holds sperm entering a female's body, and is the passage through which young are born.

Coniferous forest Land covered with trees that bear their seeds inside cones.

Crepuscular Describing animals that are active only at dawn and at dusk.

Crustaceans Water-dwelling animals that have jointed legs and a hard shell but no backbone.

Cryptic coloration Colors and often patterns on an animal that help it blend into its environment.

Cutaneous respiration Breathing through the skin

D

Deciduous forest Land covered by trees that lose their leaves during cold or dry seasons.

Direct development Process by which frog eggs develop right into froglets and skip the tadpole stage.

Diurnal Active during the day.

DNA A chain of chemical molecules that is the instruction booklet for making a living thing; scientists can tell one species from another by comparing the DNA.

E

Ectothermic Describing animals whose body temperature changes when the outside air warms up or cools down.

Embryo A developing animal that has not yet hatched or been born.

Estivation As seen in some animals, a period of inactivity during dry spells.

Explosive breeders Members of a species that breed together in a large group, usually over a very short time.

F

Fertilization The joining of egg and sperm to start development.

Filter feeder An animal that strains water for bits of food.

Foraging Searching for food.

Fossorial Living underground.

Froglet The life stage of a frog right after the tadpole stage.

G

Gill An organ for obtaining oxygen from water.

Granular glands Poison glands, which in frogs are typically in noticeable bumps, often called "warts," on the back.

H

Herbivorous Plant-eating.

Herpetologist A person who studies amphibians and reptiles.

Hibernation A state of deep sleep that some animals enter in the winter to help them survive the cold weather.

Hybrid Describing the young produced by parents of two different species.

I

Indirect development Process by which frog eggs develop first into tadpoles and then into froglets.

Infertile eggs Eggs that will never develop into young.

Introduced species An animal, plant, or other species that is brought to a new location, usually by humans, either on purpose or by accident.

Invertebrate An animal, such as an insect, spider, or earthworm, without a backbone.

L

Larva (plural, larvae) An animal in an early stage that changes form before becoming an adult.

Lateral line system A row of tiny dot- or stitch-shaped organs, seen in fishes, tadpoles, and some other water-living organisms, that allow the animal to feel vibrations in the water.

M

Marsupium Found in some animals, a pouch in the adult where the young develop.

Metamorphosis The changes in form that some animals make to become adult, such as tadpole to frog.

Microorganisms Living things that are too small to see.

Mimic To copy.

Mollusk An animal with a soft, unsegmented body that may or may not have a shell.

N

Nocturnal Active mostly at night.

Nuptial pads Seen in some frogs, thick pads that form on the forelegs, on the front feet, on the toes of the front feet, and sometimes on the chest to help the male grip onto the female during mating.

O

Ocelli In frogs, small dots of color.

Opportunistic feeder An animal that will eat just about anything that it can capture and swallow.

Ovary The organ that makes eggs.

P

Palate The roof of the mouth.

Paratoid glands In some frogs, a pair of enlarged poison-containing sacs found at the back of the head.

Permanent body of water A body of water that is filled with water year-round.

S

Silt Dirt that is washed from land and collects in rivers and streams.

Sperm Microscopic cells from a male that trigger eggs from a female to start development.

Spicules Seen on the snout of a Mesoamerican burrowing toad, small, hard, sometimes pointy bumps.

Spine Backbone; also known as the vertebral column.

Spiracle In a tadpole, a tiny hole that lets water out.

Sternum A bone in the middle of the chest between the ribs; breastbone.

Symmetrical Describing a pattern that has two sides that are mirror images of one another.

T

Temporary body of water A body of water that is only filled with water for part of the year.

Terrestrial Living on land.

Toxin Poison.

Toxicity The level of poison.

Transparent See-through.

Tubercles Bumps.

Tympanum Eardrum, which in many frogs is visible as a round spot on the side of the head.

U

Utraviolet radiation A type of light that humans cannot see, but that scientists believe may be harming some frog species, especially those that live high in mountains where the radiation is strongest.

Unken reflex Seen in some frogs and salamanders, a stiff backbend pose that serves to warn predators that the animal is bad-tasting or poisonous.

Urostyle A long, rod-shaped bone in the hip area of a frog.

V

Vernal pool A body of water that forms in the spring but then dries up for the rest of the year.

Vertebrae The bones that make up the spinal column.

Vertebrates Animals, such as birds, frogs, snakes, and mammals, with backbones.

Vocal sac Extra flesh on the throat of most male frogs that expands like a balloon when they make their calls.

W

Wart In frogs, a wart is a lump in the skin that contains poison and helps protect the frog from predators. In humans, a wart results from a virus and sometimes requires medical care.

Getting to Know Amphibians

AMPHIBIANS

Three different types of amphibians (am-FIB-ee-uhns) live on Earth today:

- Frogs are the often-slimy creatures almost everyone has seen hopping into a pond or heard calling on a spring evening. The smallest species reach less than one-half an inch (1.3 centimeters) long, while the largest can grow to more than a foot (30.5 centimeters) in length. Frogs are in the order Anura (ann-UR-uh). Toads are included in this order, too. They are simply one kind of frog. Frogs are different from other amphibians because they do not have tails when they are adults. Some frogs, called the tailed frogs, have little taillike bits of tissue, but they are not really tails. Many frogs have long and strong hind legs for hopping, but a few have short hind legs and typically get around by walking or running.

- Salamanders are the four-legged, tailed animals that hikers or gardeners sometimes surprise when they turn over a rock or log. The smallest salamanders are less than 1.2 inches (3 centimeters) long, while the largest can grow to 4 feet 11 inches (150 centimeters) in length, or more. Salamanders have bodies in the shape of a pipe with a tail at the rear. Most have small legs that are all about the same size. They hold their legs out to the side of the body when they are scrambling around on the ground. A few species have only two legs. The name of the salamanders' order is Caudata (kaw-DAY-tuh).

- Caecilians (seh-SILL-ee-uhns) come in many sizes, ranging from just 4.5 inches long to more than 5 feet 3 inches (160 centimeters) in length, but most people have never seen them in the wild. Caecilians look rather like earthworms, even having similar rings around their bodies, but caecilians have many things that earthworms do not, including jaws and teeth. A caecilian's tail is actually quite short, but since it blends into the rest of the body, this can be difficult to see unless the animal is flipped over. The tail in a caecilian begins at the vent, a slitlike opening on its underside. The caecilians are in the order Gymnophiona (jim-no-fee-OH-nuh).

In all, the world holds at least 4,837 species of frogs and toads, 502 of salamanders, and 165 of caecilians. Scientists are still discovering new species, so those numbers grow larger and larger as the years pass.

WHAT MAKES AN AMPHIBIAN AN AMPHIBIAN?

Although frogs, salamanders, and caecilians are usually not mistaken for one another, they still share several features that make them all amphibians.

Illustration of a frog skeleton. (Illustration by Marguette Dongvillo. Reproduced by permission.)

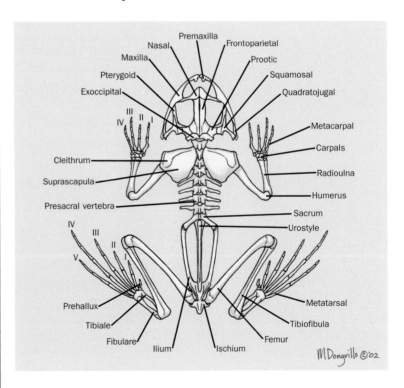

Skin

Some people confuse salamanders with lizards, but lizards are reptiles. An easy way to tell an amphibian from a reptile is to check for scales on the skin. Reptiles have scales, but amphibians do not. The skin of an amphibian is at least a little bit moist, even among the rather-dry toads, and some amphibians are very slippery. Part of the slipperiness comes from the moist or wet places they live, and part of it comes from their mucus (MYOO-kus) glands. Mucus glands are little sacks that ooze a slimy substance.

Amphibians also have another type of glands in their skin that ooze poison instead of mucus. Depending on the species, the poison may be weak or very strong. The poison in some of the poison frogs of South America is even powerful enough to kill a person who gets some in his or her bloodstream. In other species, just a little taste of the poison can turn a person's lips numb or cause extreme sickness.

Body temperature

Like fishes and reptiles, amphibians have body temperatures that become colder when the outside temperature is cold and warmer when the outside temperature is hot. Animals with a changing body temperature like this are known as ectothermic (EK-toe-thur-mik) animals. Sometimes, people call ectothermic animals "cold-blooded," but they are really only cold when the weather is also cold. Many amphibians warm themselves by sunbathing, or basking. Frogs frequently sit on shore in damp but sunny spots to bask. They may also simply swim into the warmer, upper layer of water in a pond to heat themselves up a bit. When they get too hot, they typically move to a cooler place, sometimes even going underground. This not only keeps them cooler but also helps them stay moist, which is important for their breathing.

Breathing

Amphibians breathe in several different ways. Like reptiles, birds, and mammals, most amphibians breathe in air through their nostrils to fill up their lungs. Caecilians have two lungs, but the left one is much smaller than the right one. This arrangement works well for the caecilians, which would not have room for two large lungs in their long and thin bodies. Some salamanders have very small lungs, and a few, such as the red-backed salamander that is common in North American forests, have no lungs at all.

Small or no lungs does not cause a problem for amphibians, however, because they do much of their breathing through their skin. When a person breathes in through the nose, the air travels into the lungs in the chest, where blood picks up the oxygen from the air and delivers it throughout the body. In amphibians, oxygen can pass right through their moist skin and into blood that is waiting in blood vessels just below the skin. The skin must be moist for this process to work: A dry amphibian is a dead amphibian. Using this through-the-skin breathing, which is called cutaneous respiration (kyoo-TAIN-ee-us res-per-AY-shun), amphibians can even breathe underwater. Oxygen that is dissolved in the water can also cross the skin and enter their blood.

Most amphibians go through a phase in their lives when they breathe underwater through gills, just as a fish does. Gill breathing is like cutaneous respiration, because dissolved oxygen in the water is picked up by blood in vessels that are in the gills. Gills are so full of blood vessels that they are typically bright red. Usually an amphibian breathes through gills only when it is young. Frogs, for instance, use gills when they are still tadpoles. A young salamander, which also has gills, is called a larva (LAR-vuh). The plural of larva is larvae (LAR-vee). Some amphibians, however, skip the gill-breathing phase and hatch right from the egg into a lung- and/or skin-breather. Others, however, keep their gills throughout their entire lives. Mudpuppies are examples of a salamander that has gills even as an adult. Since they live in the water, gills work well for them. In a few species, like the eastern newt, the animal goes through several phases: a gill-breathing larva, then a gill-less juvenile, and finally a gilled adult.

Hearing

Besides hearing sounds like humans do, frogs and salamanders can hear vibrations in the ground. When the ground vibrates, the movement travels up their front legs to the shoulder blade and then to a muscle that connects to the ear, so the amphibian can hear it. This type of hearing can be very sensitive. Not only can amphibians hear the footsteps of an approaching predator, like a raccoon, but they can also hear something as slight as an insect digging in the soil.

WHERE AMPHIBIANS LIVE

Amphibians live around the world. The only places where they do not live are in the extremely cold polar regions of the Earth, most of the islands in the ocean, and some desert areas. The three major groups of amphibians—the frogs, the caecilians, and the salamanders—each have their own favorite climates. Caecilians stay in warm, tropical climates and nowhere else. Although frogs live just about anywhere an amphibian can live, the greatest number of species make their homes in the tropics. Salamanders, on the other hand, tend toward cooler areas. Most salamanders live north of the Equator, and many exist in areas that have all four seasons, including a cold winter.

Because amphibians must keep their skin moist, they are always tied to water. That water may be a lake or river, a little puddle, a clammy spot under a log, or even a slightly damp burrow underground.

In the water

Most amphibians live at least part of their lives in the water. Many frogs and salamanders lay their eggs in the water. The frog eggs hatch into tadpoles, and the salamander eggs hatch into larvae. Both the tadpoles and the salamander larvae have gills that they use to breathe underwater. Eventually, the tadpoles turn into baby frogs, and the salamander larvae turn into young salamanders, and both can then leave the water to live on land. Scientists do not have all of the details about caecilians, but they think the typical caecilian lays its eggs on land; the eggs hatch into young that are also called larvae and have gills; and the larvae wriggle into water. The caecilian larvae grow in the water before losing their gills and moving onto land.

Those species that live on land for much of the year and only have their young in the water, often choose small pools that are only filled with water part of the year. Such pools are called temporary pools. Temporary pools, since they dry up later in the year, usually do not contain fish, which often eat amphibian eggs

THE RISE OF THE AMPHIBIANS

The oldest fossil amphibian is about 250 millions years old, but amphibians were around even before that. These animals lived when the Earth had only one large land mass that was surrounded by ocean. That land mass was called Pangaea (pan-JEE-uh). When Pangaea began to break up about 190 million years ago, the amphibians were split up, too. The land masses continued to move around the globe and split up into the continents as they are today. While these movements were taking place, the amphibians were changing and becoming new species. Some had features that made them well-suited to life in certain temperatures or certain areas. Today, the Earth holds thousands of different species.

and young. The only problem with laying eggs in a temporary pool is that the pools sometimes dry up too fast for the eggs to hatch into the tadpoles or larvae and for these to turn into land-living amphibians. When this happens, the young may die.

In each major group of amphibians, some species remain in the water for their entire lives. These are known as fully aquatic (uh-KWOT-ik) animals. The word *aquatic* means that an organism lives in the water, and the word *fully* means that it can always live there. Some caecilians from South America live in the water. Sirens and mudpuppies are types of salamanders that live in the water as eggs, larvae, and adults. As adults, both have bodies that are well-designed for swimming instead of walking on land. They have strong, flattened tails to move swiftly through the water but very tiny legs. The sirens only have two small front legs and have neither back legs nor hip bones.

Many frogs are fully aquatic. The clawed frogs and Surinam toads, for instance, live in just about any kind of freshwater, including swamps, slow streams, and ponds. They have very large and webbed hind feet, which make excellent paddles. One very unusual frog is the hairy frog. Adults of this species live on land most of the year, but the males will stay with the eggs underwater until they hatch. During this time, the male develops "hairs" all over the sides of its body. The hairs are actually thin fringes made of skin. This gives him more skin area and makes it easier for him to breathe. With his "hairs," he is able to stay underwater for days with his eggs without ever coming up for air.

Tadpoles, aquatic larvae, and some aquatic adult amphibians have lateral (LAT-eh-rul) line systems. Fishes have lateral line systems, too. The lateral line system looks like a row of stitch-like marks or dots that runs down each side of the body. Inside each mark or dot are tiny hairs that sway one way or the other with the movements of the water. When another animal swims past or enters the water nearby, the hairs lean and send a message to the amphibian's brain that it is not alone in the water. This helps amphibians to escape predators or, if they eat insects or other water-living prey, to find the next meal.

Along the ground

Many adult frogs and salamanders live on land and along the ground. Since they have to keep their skin moist, they often huddle under a rotting log, inside a crack in a rock, in piles of dead leaves, under the low-lying leaves of plants, or in some other damp place. Once in a while, a caecilian is also found snuggled between a leaf and stem in a low plant. In many cases, amphibians only move about on the ground during or after a heavy rain. Some, like the American toads, can survive under a bit drier conditions than other amphibians and hop or walk around the forest floor even on warm and dry summer days.

Above the ground

Some frogs and salamanders will venture into the trees. Animals that spend part of their lives off the ground and in plants or trees are known as arboreal (ar-BOR-ee-ul) animals. Among the salamanders, only some lungless salamanders are arboreal. One, which is known as the arboreal salamander, may crawl under tree bark or climb into tree holes to escape hot and dry weather. Many more frogs than salamanders are arboreal. Hundreds of these are called treefrogs and have sticky, wide pads on the tips of their toes to help them scramble up plants and trees. Some of the arboreal frogs live in humid forests that are

Life cycle of a salamander (Ambystoma opacum) and frog (Rana temporaria); a. and b.—adults; c.—eggs laid in water; d.—terrestrial salamander eggs laid in a moist area on land; e, f, g, h—larval stage; i and j—juvenile stage. (Illustration by Jacqueline Mahannah. Reproduced by permission.)

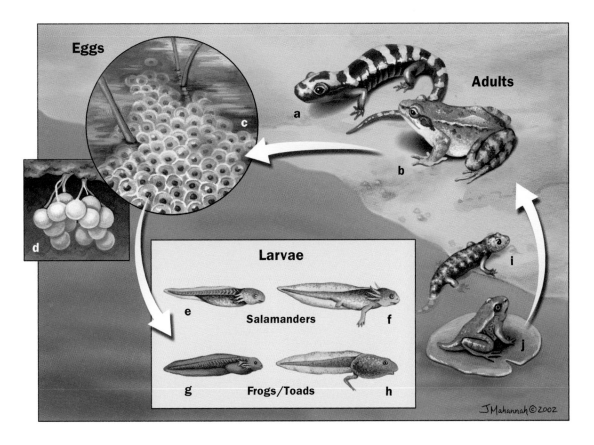

moist enough for them to sit out on leaves most of the time. Others need more moisture and find it in bromeliads (broh-MEE-lee-ads), which are plants that often grow on the sides of trees and have tube-shaped leaves that catch rainwater. There, the frogs find tiny pools where they can dip their bodies or float.

Under the soil

Since amphibians need to keep their skin moist, many of them find dampness under the soil. Animals that live underground are called fossorial (faw-SOR-ee-ul) animals. Most of the caecilians remain underground, only coming up to the surface once in a while to feed. They typically have tiny eyes and are nearly blind, although they can tell light from dark. They make their own burrows, digging headfirst into moist soil. Among the salamanders, the best-known burrowers are the mole salamanders. These salamanders, which live through much of North America, usually do not make their own burrows, instead borrowing them from mice and other small rodents. They stay inside these underground hideaways until rains wet the ground. At that time, they climb out and look for food to eat. Many of the mole salamanders, such as the blue-spotted salamander, also may live under rotting logs. The larger spotted salamander sometimes hides under rocks or deep in a damp well.

Numerous frog species, including the spadefoot toads, live underground for much of their lives. They, like many other burrowing frogs, have a hard bump that looks like the edge of a shovel blade on each of their digging feet. Some burrowing frogs do not have hard bumps on their feet. They do, however, have powerful digging legs and usually wide feet to move away the soil as they burrow.

HOW DO AMPHIBIANS MOVE?

Since amphibians may have four legs, two legs, or no legs at all, and they may spend most of their time on the ground, in the water, or in trees, they move in many different ways. Some walk or run; some hop or leap; some swim; some burrow; and some even glide through the air.

Walking and running

The land-living, or terrestrial (te-REH-stree-uhl), salamanders travel from one place to another by walking or running. They do this with their bodies very close to the ground and their upper legs held out from the body in the same position that a person takes when starting to do a push-up. Lizards, which people often confuse with salamanders, typically hold their bodies higher off the ground. The arboreal salamanders use these same movements to climb trees. Some frogs, especially those frogs with short hind legs, also get around mainly by walking. The Roraima bush toad is an example. This little toad walks slowly over the rocks where it lives. If it needs to escape quickly, it tucks in its legs so it forms a little ball and rolls off the face of the stone.

Hopping

The frogs and toads are the hoppers and leapers among the amphibians. They have two especially long ankle bones in their hind legs, as well as a long rod of bone in the hip where the jumping muscles attach. These bones give the frog's leaps added boost. They also have a strong but springy chest that can catch the frog safely as it lands on its front feet. Not all frogs and toads hop, but most do. Some, like most of the frogs in the family called true toads, have short hind legs and can only hop a short distance. Others, like most of those in the family called true frogs, have long and powerful hind legs that help them leap several times their body length. Some people even hold frog-leaping contests and bet on the frog they think will jump the farthest.

Swimming

Adult frogs swim much as they leap, shoving off with both hind feet at the same time. The frogs that are the best swimmers typically have large hind feet with webbing stretched between the toes and to the toe tips or close to the tips. Tadpoles do not have any legs until they start to turn into froglets, but they can swim by swishing their tails. Salamander larvae and the aquatic adult salamanders may or may not have tiny legs, but they all use their tails to swim. The aquatic caecilians swim much as snakes do, waving their bodies back and forth in "s" patterns to slither-swim through the water.

Burrowing

Caecilians burrow head-first into the moist soil where they live. Frogs may burrow head-first or hind feet-first. The spadefoot toads are one of the groups of frogs that dig backwards into the soil, scraping through the soil with their back feet while wriggling backward. This buries the frog deeper and deeper into the soil. The sandhill frog that lives in Australia is one of the frogs that digs head-first by paddling its front feet and making it look as if it is swimming down into the sand.

Gliding

A few of the frog species, including the flying frogs in the family known as the Asian treefrogs, can soar through the air. They do not flap their front legs or have feathers like a bird, but they do have long toes that are separated by webbing that reaches the toe tips. When they widen their toes, the feet look almost like fans. These treefrogs can leap off a tree branch high above the ground and glide safely to earth by using their fan-shaped feet to keep from falling too fast. They are also able to steer by moving their feet one way or the other.

WHAT DO AMPHIBIANS EAT?

Meat eaters

Many amphibians eat meat or are carnivorous (kar-NIH-vor-us). For most of them, their meals are insects, spiders, and other invertebrates (in-VER-teh-brehts), which are animals without backbones. Often, larger species will eat larger prey. Most caecilians eat earthworms, termites, and other invertebrates that live underground. Mexican caecilians, which may grow to 19.7 inches (500 centimeters) in length, sometimes eat other animals, such as small lizards and baby mice that crawl on top of the leaf-covered ground where the caecilians live. Most salamanders eat earthworms or small arthropods (AR-throe-pawds), which are insects and other invertebrates with jointed legs. Adult frogs also usually eat invertebrates, but if they are able to capture a larger prey and swallow it, many will. The bullfrog, which is common in much of North America, will eat anything and nearly everything from other frogs to small snakes, rodents, and even small birds.

Many amphibians hunt by ambush, which means that they stay very still and wait for a prey animal to happen by. Some amphibians hunt by foraging (FOR-ij-ing), when they crawl, hop, or swim about looking for something to eat. Many amphibians simply snap their mouths around the prey and swallow it. Some flick their tongues out to nab it and then reel their tongues and the prey back into their mouths. Many salamanders have especially long tongues.

Plant eaters

Tadpoles are usually herbivorous (urh-BIH-vor-us), which means that they eat plants. Many have beaklike mouths that scrape algae (AL-jee) and other scum from rocks and underwater plants. Some, like the tadpoles of spadefoot toads, will eat invertebrates in addition to plants.

AMPHIBIANS AS PREY

A wide variety of animals attack and eat amphibians. Birds, snakes, raccoons and other mammals, fishes, and other amphibians are their predators. Even insects, like diving beetles, can kill a tadpole. For most amphibians, the best defense against their predators is to remain still and let their camouflage colors help them stay out of sight. Frogs, in particular, are often the same color as their surroundings. Some, like the horned frogs,

Amphibian behavioral and physiological defense mechanisms; a. Marine toad (Bufo marinus) inflates its lungs and enlarges; b. Two-lined salamander (Eurycea bislineata) displays tail autotomy (tail is able to detach); c. Eleutherodactylus curtipes feigns death; d. Echinotriton andersoni protrudes its ribs; e. Bombina frog displays unken reflex. (Illustration by Jacqueline Mahannah. Reproduced by permission.)

have large and pointy heads that look much like dead leaves. Other amphibians are very brightly colored. The juvenile eastern newt, for example, is bright orange red. This newt also is very poisonous, and its bright colors advertise to predators that they are dangerous to eat.

When numerous amphibians are attacked, they will stiffen their bodies, arch their backs, and hold out their feet. This position is called the unken (OONK-en) reflex. The fire-bellied frogs use this position, which shows off their bright red, yellow, or orange undersides and the similarly colored bottoms of their feet. The colors may remind predators that these frogs have a bad-tasting poison in their skin and convince them to leave the frogs alone.

Although it is not very common, some amphibians will fight back if attacked. Adult African bullfrogs will snap at large predators, even lions or people, who come too close to the frogs or their young. Among salamanders, the large hellbenders can give a painful bite.

REPRODUCTION

In all three groups of amphibians, mating involves both males and females. The females produce the eggs, and the males make a fluid that contains microscopic cells called sperm. An egg will only develop into a baby amphibian if it mixes with sperm. This mixing is called fertilization (FUR-tih-lih-ZAY-shun). In almost all frogs, the male climbs onto the back of the female, and as she lays her eggs, he releases his fluid so that the eggs are fertilized outside. In the caecilians, the male adds his fluid to the eggs while they are still inside the female's body. Salamanders fall in between these two types of fertilization. In most salamanders, the male puts drops of his fluid along the ground, and the female follows along behind to scoop up the droplets and put them inside her body with the eggs. All amphibians either lay their eggs in the water or in a moist place where the eggs will not dry out.

Most amphibian eggs hatch into tadpoles or larvae before becoming miniature versions of the adults. Often, these eggs, tadpoles, and larvae develop in the water. In some species, the adults lay the eggs on land but near water; the eggs hatch into tadpoles or larvae that squirm into the water or scramble onto the parent's back for a ride to the water. A number of species have young that never enter the water. In many of these amphibians,

the eggs skip the tadpole or larvae stage and hatch right into miniature adults.

ACTIVITY PERIODS

Amphibians often have certain times of day or times of year when they are active. Some may even enter states of deep sleep for parts of the year when the weather is too cold or too dry.

Day and night

Most amphibians are nocturnal (nahk-TER-nuhl), which means they are active at night. Nocturnal animals hide someplace during the day. Sirens, which are the two-legged salamanders, spend their days buried in mud. Many frogs likewise stay out of sight during the day, sometimes hidden underground, in a rock crevice, or in some other hiding place, and come out at night to look for food or to mate. By being active at night instead of the daytime, these amphibians can avoid many predators that rely on their eyesight to find prey. Nights are also usually more humid than days, so the amphibians can keep their skin moist better if they are only active at night.

These aglypto frogs are engaging in a behavior known as "explosive breeding." (Photograph by Harald Schüetz. Reproduced by permission.)

Some species are diurnal (die-UR-nuhl), which means that they are active during the day. In many cases, these species have especially poisonous or bad-tasting skin that protects them from daytime predators. Many of the poison frogs of South America, for example, are diurnal. On rainy days, some of the nocturnal amphibians will come out of hiding and wander about. With the wet weather, they can keep their skin moist.

During the seasons

Many species of amphibians are active only during some times of year. Those that live in climates with a cold winter often spend the winter underground or in another sheltered spot and enter a state of deep sleep, called hibernation (high-bur-NAY-shun). The bodies of some species, like the wood frog in the family of true frogs, actually freeze in the winter, but they are able to thaw out the following spring and continue living. Many other cold-climate species become active again when the spring arrives. Salamanders in the northern United States, for instance, start to move about on land even before the snow melts. Frequently, in these species, the spring also is the time for mating.

Besides the cold-weather species, some other amphibians enter a state of deep sleep when the weather becomes too dry. For species that live in deserts or dry grasslands, such as the water-holding frog of Australia, many burrow down into the ground and wait there until the next rainy season arrives. A period of deep sleep during a dry period is known as estivation (es-tih-VAY-shun). In these species, the rainy season marks the beginning of the mating period.

Amphibians that live in warm and wet tropical areas usually are active all year long, but they often mate only on rainy days.

AMPHIBIANS AND PEOPLE

Of all the amphibians, frogs are the most familiar to people. Nearly everyone has seen a frog or heard one calling during its mating season. Because neither salamanders nor caecilians have mating calls, and both usually stay out of sight during the day, many people have seen few, if any, of these two types of animals. Frogs are also much more common pets than salamanders or caecilians. In addition, many people eat frogs and some even eat tadpoles, but few people eat caecilians or salamanders.

Scientists are interested in amphibians for many reasons. In some species, their skin poisons or other chemical compounds have been made into or studied as medicines. Scientists also use amphibians to learn how their bodies work and therefore learn more about how human bodies function. Perhaps most importantly, ecologists see amphibians as living alert systems. Since amphibians live on land and in the water, and often are very sensitive to changes in the environment, they are excellent alarms that can warn humans about problems, such as water or air pollution.

ENDANGERED AMPHIBIANS

Through the World Conservation Union, which goes by the initials IUCN, scientists keep track of how well amphibians, along with other organisms, are surviving on Earth. They separate the species into different categories based on the number of individuals in the species and anything that might make them lose or gain numbers in the future. One of the categories the IUCN uses is called Data Deficient. This category means that scientists do not have enough information to make a judgment about the threat of extinction. The number of amphibians listed as Data Deficient is quite large: 1,165 species of frogs, 62 species of salamanders, and 111 caecilians. Many of these species are rare and/or live underground or in some other hard-to-reach location where they are difficult to study.

Amphibians in danger

The IUCN lists 367 species of frogs and forty-seven species of salamanders as Critically Endangered and facing an extremely high risk of extinction in the wild; 623 frog species, 106 salamanders, and one caecilian are Endangered and facing a very high risk of extinction in the wild; 544 frogs, 86 salamander species, and three caecilians are Vulnerable and facing a high risk of extinction in the wild; and 302 frogs and fifty-nine salamanders are Near Threatened and at risk of becoming threatened with extinction in the future.

Many of these species are at risk because the places where they live or breed are disappearing or changing, perhaps as

EXTRA LEGS?

In 1995, a group of students at the Minnesota New Country School were outside hiking when they found frogs with odd legs, including extra feet. In all, half of the frogs they saw had some type of deformity. After this discovery, many other people began reporting other deformed frogs. Scientists immediately started tests and experiments to learn why the frogs were deformed. Today, many believe the deformities were the result of disease, pollution, and/or some of the sun's rays, called UV radiation.

Amphibian morphological defense mechanisms; a. Darwin's frog (*Rhinoderma darwinii*) uses camouflage and cryptic structure; b. *Pseudotriton ruber* and *Notophthalmus viridescens* display mimicry; c. *Bufo americanus* has poison parotid glands; d. Poison dart frog (*Dendrobates pumilio*) has warning coloration; e. *Physalaemus nattereri* has eye spots on its hind quarters. (Illustration by Jacqueline Mahannah. Reproduced by permission.)

people cut down trees for lumber or otherwise clear the land to put in farms, homes, or other buildings. Some of the other problems for amphibians come from air and water pollution, infection with a fungus that is killing amphibians around the world, and global warming. Global warming changes weather patterns, sometimes causing especially dry conditions in some places. Since frogs need to keep their skin moist, especially dry weather can be deadly to them.

Saving endangered amphibians

To help many of the at-risk amphibians, governments, scientific organizations, and other groups are protecting some of the areas where the animals live. These may be national parks, preserves, or other natural areas. Many local, state, and national governments have also designed laws to protect the amphibians from being hunted or collected. In a few cases, conservationists are trying to raise amphibians in captivity and then releasing them into the wild with the hopes that they will survive, breed, and increase the size of the natural populations.

Too late to save

The efforts to protect the Earth's amphibians are important, because many species have already become extinct in recent years. An extinct species is one that is no longer in existence.

Leopard frogs with missing, deformed or extra legs started appearing near St. Albans Bay of Lake Champlain in St. Albans, Vermont. Biologists are not sure if pollution, a parasite, disease, or something else is causing the frogs to develop abnormally. Photograph AP/World Wide Photos. Reproduced by permission.

This includes two species of salamanders and thirty-two species of frogs. In addition, the IUCN lists one frog as Extinct in the Wild, which means that it is no longer alive except in captivity or through the aid of humans.

FOR MORE INFORMATION

Books:

Behler, John. *Simon and Schuster's Guide to Reptiles and Amphibians of the World.* New York: Simon and Schuster, 1989, 1997.

Clarke, Barry. *Amphibian.* New York: Dorling Kindersley, 1993.

Florian, Douglas. *Discovering Frogs.* New York: Charles Scribner's Sons, 1986.

Halliday, Tim, and Kraig Adler, eds. *The Encyclopedia of Reptiles and Amphibians (Smithsonian Handbooks).* New York: Facts On File, 1991.

Harding, J. H. *Amphibians and Reptiles of the Great Lakes Region.* Ann Arbor: The University of Michigan Press Institution Press, 1997.

Lamar, William. *The World's Most Spectacular Reptiles and Amphibians.* Tampa, FL: World Publications, 1997.

Maruska, Edward. *Amphibians: Creatures of the Land and Water.* New York: Franklin Watts, 1994.

Miller, Sara Swan. *Frogs and Toads: The Leggy Leapers.* New York: Franklin Watts, 2000.

O'Shea, Mark, and Tim Halliday. *Smithsonian Handbooks: Reptiles and Amphibians (Smithsonian Handbooks).* New York: Dorling Kindersley Publishing, 2002.

Periodicals:

Hogan, Dan, and Michele Hogan. "Freaky Frogs: Worldwide Something Weird Is Happening to Frogs." *National Geographic Explorer* (March–April 2004): 10.

Masibay, Kim Y. "Rainforest Frogs: Vanishing Act? Frog Populations Around the World Are Dying Off Mysteriously. Can Scientists Save Them—Before It's Too Late?" *Science World* (March 11, 2002): 12.

Sunquist, Fiona. "The Weird World of Frogs." *National Geographic World* (March 2002): 14.

Walters, Mark Jerome. "Spotting the Smallest Frog: As Hopes Fade for One Species, a Tiny Frog Comes into View." *Animals* (May–June 1997): 8.

Web sites:

"North American Reporting Center for Amphibian Malformations." *National Biological Information Infrastructure.* http://frogweb.nbii.gov/narcam/index.html (accessed on May 15, 2005).

Stoddard, Tim. "Island hoppers: Sri Lankan tree frogs end game of hide-and-seek." *BU Bridge.* http://www.bu.edu/bridge/archive/2002/10-18/frogs.htm (accessed on February 12, 2005).

Trivedi, Bijal P. "Frog Fathers Provide Transport, Piggyback Style." *National Geographic Today.* http://news.nationalgeographic.com/news/2002/08/0807_020807_TVfrogs.html (accessed on February 12, 2005).

"Weird Frog Facts." *Frogland.* http://allaboutfrogs.org/weird/weird.html (accessed on February 12, 2005).

LEPTODACTYLID FROGS

Leptodactylidae

Class: Amphibia

Order: Anura

Family: Leptodactylidae

Number of species: 1,124 species

PHYSICAL CHARACTERISTICS

With more than 1,100 species of leptodactylid frogs, this is a huge family that has many different-looking species. The smallest species grow only to 0.4 inches (1 centimeter) long from the tip of the snout to the back of the rump, while female helmeted water toads can reach as much as 12.8 inches (32 centimeters) long. Many species in this family have toadlike features, including short legs and warty backs, while others have the look of a typical frog with long, jumping hind legs and smooth skin on their backs. Some have chunky bodies, some are slender, and a few are quite flat. Some of the more unusual members of this family have very baggy skin that hangs in folds from their sides and the upper part of each hind leg, and others have fleshy points, or "horns," on the eyelids.

Although they may look different on the outside, they do share some common features. For example, most of the leptodactylid frogs have teeth on the upper jaw, as well as horizontal pupils in their eyes. A few have vertical pupils. The bones at the tips of the toes of all species in this family either are T-shaped or have knobs. In some species, small pads cover the tips and help the frog to climb up slippery rocks or tall trees. Most species in this family are gray, green, or brown and blend into the background.

A few, however, have bright patterns. The gold-striped frog, for instance, is black with bright yellow stripes. Scientists think that these bright colors trick predators into thinking the gold-striped frog is actually a species of poison dart frog that is also

phylum

class

subclass

order

monotypic order

suborder

▲ **family**

black with yellow stripes. Predators will not eat the poison dart frog, because it oozes a poison from its skin, and may also avoid the look-alike species, even though it is harmless. In addition to its copycat color, the gold-striped frog has red "flash colors" at the tops of its legs. When threatened, this frog and some other species in the family that have similar bright patches move their legs so these spots show. This sudden burst of color may surprise a predator and give the frog time to escape. The gray four-eyed frog has another feature on its back that can scare off attackers. When threatened, it rounds its lower back to show off two large, dark-colored glands. This display gives the impression that a larger animal with two big eyes has suddenly appeared.

Males and females usually look alike. In some species, however, the males develop spines on the front toes and/or chest during the breeding season. These spines help the male ride piggyback and hold onto the female during mating. The males of many species in this family grab the female around her front legs, but some hold her near her back legs while she lays her eggs.

GEOGRAPHIC RANGE

These frogs live in North, Central, and South America, as well as the West Indies. In North America, they can be found in Mexico and southernmost parts of the United States. One species, the gray four-eyed frog, lives farther south than any other species in the world: the Straits of Magellan at the southern tip of South America.

HABITAT

These frogs may live almost anywhere from hot and humid valleys and lowland forests to cooler, drier land high up in the mountains. Depending on the species, they may spend much of their time hiding under rocks or other places on land, hopping through grass or forests, climbing in trees, or swimming under water. Some even live in burrows inside ant hills. Mating in the typical leptodactylid frog happens in the water. This may be a lake, small pond, a pool that is only filled with water during part of the year, or some other body of water.

DIET

Most of the species in this family get their food by finding a promising spot and waiting there for a meal to come to them. This kind of sit-and-wait method is called ambush hunting.

Many of the species in this family have colors and patterns that make them almost disappear from view if they remain very still. Many leptodactylid frogs eat arthropods (AR-thro-pawds), which are spiders, insects, and other invertebrates with jointed legs. An invertebrate (in-VER-teh-breht) is an animal without a backbone. Some of the larger species, like the Surinam horned frog and South American bullfrog, will eat almost anything that they can capture and swallow, including other frogs, snakes, and even small birds and mammals.

BEHAVIOR AND REPRODUCTION

Although some species in this family are active during the daytime, most of them usually stay out of sight while the sun is shining and move about after dark. During the day, they typically hide under rocks or logs, inside dark cracks and burrows, or tucked into the leaves of plants. Some of the species, like the Surinam horned frog, have camouflage colors and eyebrow "horns" that help the frog to look like a leaf when it is nestled in a pile of dead leaves on the ground. Most leptodactylid frogs do their hunting at night.

To protect themselves against predators, the majority of the frogs in this family simply try to hop away. Others will stay still and hope their camouflage is good enough to keep them hidden. If an attacker comes too close, some species will use other defensive methods. For example, the helmeted water toad takes a big gulp of air to blow up its body, stands up as tall as possible on all four legs, opens wide its mouth, and snaps at the attacker. Since males of this species can reach 4.8 inches (12 centimeters) long, and females can grow to a whopping 12.8 inches (32 centimeters), they can convince many predators to back off.

Some leptodactylid frogs that live in areas with particularly dry seasons survive the weather by burrowing into the mud left on the bottom of disappearing pools of water. Budgett's frog is an example. It digs deep in the mud until it is completely covered, then sheds its outer layers of skin, which it wears like a blanket around its body. The dead skin cocoon helps the frog to stay moist inside during the dry period, which may last many weeks. When the rainy season returns, the water drenches the ground, softens up the cocoon, and the frog crawls out of its burrow.

Many of the frogs that live in climates with both dry and wet seasons mate in the rainy season. Some of those that live in areas that are wet and warm all year may mate during only a

NOISE POLLUTION—FROM A FROG?

Until recently, no frogs lived in Hawaii. When the 2- to 2.5-inch-long frog, called the Puerto Rican coqui, hitchhiked to Hawaii in some plants, it found a good place to live and multiply. It started to do what it does naturally: After the sun sets, the males performed their two-part calls: koh-kee, koh-kee. People in Hawaii, however, were used to a quieter night, and some soon began complaining about the "racket" from the frogs, claiming that it disturbed their sleep and would possibly turn away island visitors. Despite their grumbles, the frog still lives in Hawaii and is doing well there.

short time each year, or they may mate off and on all year long. Regardless of when they mate, they kick off a mating period with the calls of the males. Some, like the Cururu lesser escuerzo, call from water, but Perez's snouted frog and others call from their hiding places on land. Some males, including gray four-eyed frogs, do not call. When a female approaches, the male typically climbs onto her back and hangs on by either clinging to her at her front legs or in front of her hind legs. This piggyback position is called amplexus (am-PLEK-sus). Those frog pairs that are on land hop and crawl over to the water. Those that are already in the water mate there. While the male is still on her back, the female lays her eggs.

The females of some species, like the warty tree toad, drop their eggs in the water, and they develop into tadpoles there. Other species, like the Túngara frog, lay their eggs in foam nests. Depending on the species, one or both adults make the nest by using their hind legs to whip up the eggs, water, and some mucus from their bodies until it turns into a frothy foam. The eggs hatch into tadpoles inside the foam. Depending on the species, the tadpoles may leave the nest and turn into froglets in the water, or they may stay inside and make the change inside the nest. The females of few species in this family, including the Puerto Rican coqui, mate and lay their eggs in plants that grow in trees. In the case of the Puerto Rican coqui, the male then takes charge of the nest, often sitting on top of them. These eggs skip the tadpole stage and hatch right into froglets. The golden coqui is the only member of the family to give birth to froglets. Instead of laying her eggs, the female keeps them inside her body, where they hatch into froglets. She then gives birth to the live young. The females in some species lay a few dozen eggs, but others can lay hundreds at a time. Usually the biggest frogs have the greatest number of eggs.

LEPTODACTYLID FROGS AND PEOPLE

People hunt a few of the larger leptodactylid frogs for food and sometimes collect them and some of the pretty smaller species for the pet trade. Introduced coqui frogs have made the news in Hawaii. Hidden inside plants shipped to Hawaii from their native lands, coquis have found their new home to be a good place to live and raise families, but some people there are less pleased with the new arrivals. They complain about the male frogs' loud mating calls.

CONSERVATION STATUS

Of the 1,124 species in this family, the World Conservation Union (IUCN) lists two as Extinct, which means they are no longer in existence; 133 are Critically Endangered and facing an extremely high risk of extinction in the wild; 209 are Endangered and at very high risk of extinction in the wild; 133 are Vulnerable and facing a high risk of extinction in the wild; 60 are Near Threatened and at risk of becoming threatened with extinction in the future; and 249 are Data Deficient, which means not enough information is available to make a judgment about the threat of extinction.

Surinam horned frog *(Ceratophrys cornuta)*

SURINAM HORNED FROG
Ceratophrys cornuta

Physical characteristics: Also known as the horned frog, Amazonian horned frog, or packman frog, the Surinam horned frog is a large, fat-looking frog. Its round, rather flat body has the shape of a doughnut without the hole. Its wide head has an immense mouth that stretches from one side to the other, light tan eyes, and pointy eyebrows that resemble little horns. The body, which has small, scattered, cone-shaped warts across the back and down the sides, is green to yellowish green. Its back is patterned with brown, blotchy stripes, and a thin, brown band runs across the head from one eyebrow horn

to the other. The frog usually sits with its rather small hind legs tucked up against the body and its short but thick front legs held pigeon-toed, or facing inward. Both its front and hind legs are lime green with brown to dark green bands. The toes on the front feet are un-webbed, while those on the hind feet are partly webbed. The belly is smooth and cream-colored, and the throat is dark brown to black. Males and females look alike except during the mating season, when the males develop rough pads on the inner toe of each front foot. Adult females can grow to as much as 4.7 inches (12.0 centimeters) long from snout to rump. The males are smaller, reaching 3.1 inches (8.0 centimeters) in length.

Geographic range: The Surinam horned frog lives in the Amazon Basin, which is a large, low area of northern South America. In this region, heavy rains, small creeks, and streams all eventually drain into Amazon River. It also can be found in the small countries of French Guiana, Guyana, and Suriname.

Habitat: During most of the year, the horned frog stays on land and among the thick plants of the rainforest floor. In the breeding season, however, it moves into small pools of water, which may or may not dry up later in the season.

Diet: The Surinam horned frog is an opportunistic (ah-per-too-NIS-tik) hunter, which means that it will eat just about anything that it can grab and swallow. Prey includes grasshoppers and other insects, spiders, other frogs, and even quite large animals like snakes, lizards, and mice. The tadpoles, which have a long tooth-like poker on the bottom jaw, are also good hunters. They eat tadpoles, including other Surinam horned frog tadpoles, by opening their mouths and sucking them in. With a chomp of the jaws, the poker spears the prey, and the tadpole quickly swallows it.

Behavior and reproduction: Although it is a large frog, the Surinam horned frog can do quite a vanishing act. The ground of the rainforest is cluttered with growing plants and mounds of fallen leaves. This frog hops to such a mound, shuffles its body back and forth until all but its head is buried in the leaves, and then stops moving. With its pointy eyebrows that look like the edges of curled leaves and its camouflage colors, the frog nearly disappears. From here, it can watch for prey animals to walk unknowingly past. When one approaches closely enough, the frog lunges out, opens its immense mouth, and snaps it up. The frog may continue this style of sit-and-wait hunting, called ambush hunting, for several days from the same spot. It usually waits until dark on a rainy night to move to a new place.

Breeding season for this species is short, with all of the frogs mating and laying eggs when the first, heavy spring storms soak the land. The males hop to pools of water, sit on the edges, and make their deep calls. Some people describe the call as sounding like the "moo" of a cow or the "baa" of a sheep. When a female responds to a male's call, he climbs onto her back and hangs on by her front legs. The female lays up to 2,000 small eggs in the water. The eggs develop into tadpoles, which grow to about 2.5 inches (6.5 centimeters) long from head to tail before changing into froglets.

Surinam horned frogs and people: People see this frog more often in the pet store than in the wild.

Conservation status: The World Conservation Union (IUCN) does not consider this species to be at risk. Some of the areas where this frog lives are protected places, such as refuges and parks, but some are not. As more forests are logged and otherwise cleared, this frog's habitat is shrinking. ■

Budgett's frog *(Lepidobatrachus laevis)*

BUDGETT'S FROG
Lepidobatrachus laevis

Physical characteristics: With a body that is shaped like a flat, round pillow and a mouth that reaches almost from front leg to front leg, Budgett's frog is an odd-looking animal. Its head is extremely wide and has no noticeable neck to tell where the head ends and the back begins. It has two cream-colored eyes with round pupils. The eyes are set close together on top of its flat head with two nostrils below and between them on its rounded snout. Compared to its body, the four legs are quite short. The toes on its front feet are unwebbed, but those on the rear feet have webs almost to the tips. Each hind foot also has a large, black, shovel-like bump, or tubercle (TOO-ber-kul), that the

frog uses for burrowing. Budgett's frog has an olive brown to gray back with dark blotches or pale streaks. Its underside is white. A large frog, adults usually grow to be 4.5 to 5.1 inches (11 to 13 centimeters) long from snout to rump.

Geographic range: Budgett's frog lives in the Chaco Region, a dry part of northern Argentina, southern Paraguay, and the southern half of Bolivia, which are located in central South America.

Habitat: During most of the year, Budgett's frog digs burrows in dry scrub areas and stays underground. In the breeding season, however, it comes on land and moves into shallow pools of water that dry up later in the year.

Diet: The adult diet includes snails and smaller frogs, which it finds in its pool of water. The tadpoles are also meat-eaters and eat other smaller tadpoles, which they swallow in one gulp.

Behavior and reproduction: Budgett's frog's life cycle is tied to the weather. During the long, dry season, it remains underground in burrows, but during the rainy season, it climbs onto land and into the water, where it will mate and eat a year's worth of food. After the rains end and the land begins to dry up, the frog starts digging, using its shovel-like tubercles to burrow backward into the mud on the bottom of its one-time watering hole. When it is well underground, it stops digging and sheds the outer layer of its skin. It sheds several times, and each time, the peeled-off skin piles up around the frog's body, forming a coat, or cocoon, of dead skin. This cocoon, which is waterproof, helps the frog stay moist inside. Without it, the surrounding dirt would soon soak up the frog's moisture and dry out and kill the animal.

The frog stays in its protective cocoon for about nine months when the spring rains come and wet the land again. As the water soaks the soil, the cocoon softens, and the frog crawls out of its burrow, dragging the cocoon around its body. Before doing much else, it eats its cocoon. The frog is then active for about three months—November, December, and January, which are spring and summer months in South America. If a predator approaches one of these large frogs, it faces the attacker and opens wide its gigantic mouth. In many cases, this is enough to convince the predator to find something else to eat. Once the frog becomes active in the spring, breeding starts soon. The males float in shallow pools of water and squeal their calls. Females respond, and each male mates by climbing onto a female's back and holding onto her near her front legs. A single female can lay 1,200 eggs at a time. The eggs sink in water and hatch into tadpoles in less than a day. In about 20 days, the already 2-inch-long (5.1-centimeter-long) tadpoles turn into froglets.

Budgett's frogs and people: People rarely see these frogs in the wild. They are not popular in the pet trade.

Conservation status: The IUCN does not consider this species to be at risk, but its populations in Argentina have begun to disappear. Scientists are unsure why. ■

Rock River frog *(Thoropa miliaris)*

ROCK RIVER FROG
Thoropa miliaris

Physical characteristics: The Rock River frog has a typical frog shape: long hind legs with long toes, shorter front legs and toes, and a slender body and head with large, bulging eyes. The toes on its un-webbed front and back feet end in slightly widened tips. Eardrums show on each side of its rather wide head, just behind the rust-colored eyes. The frog is tan to reddish brown on its head, back, and legs, often with a noticeable dark stripe on each side of the body and running from almost the tip of the rounded snout to the start of the back leg. Its hind legs have dark brown to black bands. Its front legs have less banding. Its belly is gray, and it has a yellowish color at the

tops of its hind legs. Males and females usually look alike, but in the breeding season, the males develop tiny spines on three of the front toes on each foot. Males are also slightly smaller than females. Females grow to 3.2 inches (8.1 centimeters) long from snout to rump, while males reach 2.8 inches (7.1 centimeters) in length.

Geographic range: It lives in a small area of southeastern Brazil near the Atlantic coast.

Habitat: It lives in warm and moist forests, especially along streams.

Diet: The Rock River frog probably eats arthropods, as do many of the other species in this family.

Behavior and reproduction: The Rock River frog becomes active at night, when it hops about on land looking for food. In the breeding season, the males climb onto streamside rocks and call. When females follow the calls to the males, they mate, and the females lay their eggs in the water. The eggs hatch into tadpoles, which use their long, strong tails to swim to the shoreline and up onto wet rocks.

Rock River frogs and people: People rarely see this species. It is not common in the pet trade.

Conservation status: The IUCN does not consider this species to be at risk, but it does live in areas where the habitat may disappear due to the cutting of trees and plants and the construction of buildings and dams. Scientists are also watching it to see whether a fungus that is killing off many different types of frogs worldwide may affect this species, too. ■

Perez's snouted frog *(Edalorhina perezi)*

PEREZ'S SNOUTED FROG
Edalorhina perezi

Physical characteristics: Perez's snouted frog has a dark brown to black stripe running along each side and separating its gray or brown back and head from its bright white underside. Its head has a rounded snout and two tan or gray and copper eyes are outlined on top with thin, finger-like bumps that look almost like long eyelashes. Its white belly has black markings, and its back has ridges that stretch from the back of the head to the rump. The back also sometimes has reddish brown stripes. Females are slightly larger than the males and grow to 1.4 inches (3.5 centimeters) long from snout to rump. The males reach 1.2 inches (3 centimeters) in length.

During the daytime, Perez's snouted frog hops through the piles of leaves on the rainforest floor and looks for things to eat. It relies on the dead-leaf colors of its head and back to hide it from predators. (Illustration by Dan Erickson. Reproduced by permission)

Geographic range: It lives in the Amazon River basin from southern Colombia to northern Bolivia.

Habitat: Perez's snouted frog lives in valleys and other low-lying areas of the wet and warm tropical rainforests. They breed in small pools of water, usually those that dry up later in the year.

Diet: The adult diet includes flies, crickets, and other insects, as well as spiders and other arthropods.

Behavior and reproduction: During the daytime, this frog hops through the piles of leaves on the rainforest floor and looks for things to eat. It relies on the dead-leaf colors of its head and back to hide it from the scanning eyes of predators. In the breeding season, each of the males begins to call from his spot in the leaves. When a female approaches, the male climbs on her back and hangs on near her front legs as they scuttle off to a pool of water. There, the female lays 78 to 98 eggs. The male and female together beat the water, eggs, and fluid from their bodies into foam, which floats on top of the water. In four to six days, the eggs hatch into tadpoles, which swim out of the foam nest into the water. The tadpoles have tan backs and greenish yellow bellies and can grow to about 0.8 inches (2 centimeters) before turning into froglets.

Perez's snouted frogs and people: People rarely see this species. It is not common in the pet trade.

Conservation status: The IUCN does not consider this common species to be at risk. While some of its habitat is disappearing as people move into the area or turn the forests into farmland, these frogs seem to be doing very well in the wild.   ■

South American bullfrog *(Leptodactylus pentadactylus)*

SOUTH AMERICAN BULLFROG
Leptodactylus pentadactylus

Physical characteristics: A large frog, the male South American bullfrog can grow to 7.3 inches (18 centimeters) long from snout to rump, while the female usually reaches 6.9 inches (17.6 centimeters) in length. It has a typical frog body with long, jumping hind legs, and shorter front legs. Its large head has a rounded snout with brown triangular patches on the upper lip, large eyes, and a noticeable ear drum on each side. Its head and back are usually tan to reddish brown, and two ridges run from the back of the head to the rump. Sometimes, the frog has reddish brown markings between the two ridges. The

A large frog, the male South American bullfrog can grow to 7.3 inches (18 centimeters) long from snout to rump, while the female usually reaches 6.9 inches (17.6 centimeters) in length. (Illustration by Dan Erickson. Reproduced by permission.)

front and back legs often have dark brown bands running across them. The toes on all four feet are unwebbed. Its underside is cream-colored with black or dark brown markings. For most of the year, the male and female look similar. During breeding season, however, the male's front legs swell, the inside toe on each front foot grows a spine, and two spines develop on each side of the chest. The large front legs and the spines help the male hold onto the female during mating.

Geographic range: This frog is found in Central and South America. It reaches as far north as Honduras in Central America and in much of northern South America, including the central and northern Amazon River basin, and parts of Ecuador and the Guianas.

Habitat: The South American bullfrog lives mainly in lowland rainforests, but it sometimes makes it home in drier forests and even slightly up the sides of mountains but below 3,800 feet (1,200 meters) above sea level. During breeding season, they move into slow-moving streams and ponds.

Diet: South American bullfrogs will eat almost anything. Adults eat large arthropods, frogs and other reptiles, and small mammals and birds. The younger bullfrogs tend to eat smaller arthropods. Tadpoles are both vegetarians and meat-eaters, gobbling up plants as well as frog eggs and tadpoles. They will even eat their own young relatives.

Behavior and reproduction: During the day, this frog hides under logs, inside burrows, or underneath leaf piles on land. Although this behavior protects it from being seen, predators sometimes spot the frog. To protect itself, the frog tries something different. It sucks in air to blow itself up to a larger size and stands as tall as it can on all four legs. The frog can also release a bad-tasting poison from its skin. Finally, as a last resort, the South American bullfrog often screams with a high voice when an attacker picks it up.

During breeding season, each male hops to water, either to the edge of a pond or a slow offshoot of a stream, and makes his loud, repeating "whoorup" calls. When a female arrives, he scoots onto her back and grasps her near her front legs. As she lays her 1,000 or so eggs, he flails his legs to whip up a foam nest. The nest lies in a dip in the ground just beyond the edge of the water. The eggs hatch into brown tadpoles about two or three days later. When rains come, the water floods the nest, and the tadpoles swim out and into the stream or pond. The tadpoles grow quickly, reaching 3.3 inches (8.3 centimeters) long, and turn into froglets when they are about a month old.

South American bullfrogs and people: Local people in some areas eat these frogs.

Conservation status: The IUCN does not consider this species to be at risk, although it is becoming rather rare in some areas where it is hunted as food. ■

Gold-striped frog (*Lithodytes lineatus*)

GOLD-STRIPED FROG
Lithodytes lineatus

Physical characteristics: True to its name, the gold-striped frog has two golden yellow stripes, each one running from its rounded snout above the brown eye and eardrum and down its slender, slightly warty back to the rump. Its legs are tan with black bands, often faded on the front legs, and end in unwebbed toes that are tipped with small pads. Small red blotches show at the top of the hind legs. The frog's smooth underside is light grayish brown. Males and females look alike, although the females are slightly larger. Females can reach 2.2 inches (5.6 centimeters) long from snout to rump, while males grow to 1.8 inches (4.5 centimeters) in length.

Geographic range: This frog is found in the Amazon River basin of northern South America, as well as in the Guianas.

Habitat: For most of the year, gold-striped frogs are found in hot, moist, low-lying rainforests.

Diet: Adults search the forest floor for earthworms and arthropods to eat.

Behavior and reproduction: Although young gold-striped frogs may hop about on land in the daytime and at night, the adults usually go out only after dark. In the daylight, the adults hide from sight in underground burrows, sometimes inside the nests of leaf-cutting ants. During breeding times, the males call from their daytime getaways. When a female approaches the male, he hops onto her back, and they head for water. She lays about 200 eggs inside a foam nest that they make near the edge of the water. The eggs hatch into tadpoles, which stay inside the nest for about one to two weeks, and then swim off into the water. In about nine weeks, when the bright pink tadpoles are as much as 2 inches (5 centimeters) long, they turn into froglets.

Gold-striped frogs and people: People often mistake this species for a poison dart frog. While poison dart frogs ooze what can be dangerous poison from their skin, the gold-striped frogs do not.

Conservation status: This common species is not considered endangered or threatened. ■

Gray four-eyed frog *(Pleurodema bufonina)*

GRAY FOUR-EYED FROG
Pleurodema bufonina

Physical characteristics: The gray four-eyed frog gets its name from the two, large, dark-colored glands on its hips. When looking at the frog from the back end, the glands look somewhat like oval-shaped eyes. This species has a short, rounded snout, small eardrums, short and chubby front legs that have unwebbed toes, and longer hind legs with slightly webbed toes. Its upper body is brown, sometimes with darker brown spots and often with a thin, light stripe down the middle of the back. Its underside is light tan. Males and females look alike, but females are a bit larger. Females grow to 2.2 inches

(5.6 centimeters) from snout to rump, while males can reach 1.8 inches (4.5 centimeters) in length.

Geographic range: This frog lives farther south than any other frog in the world. It makes its home in Chile and nearby parts of western Argentina, including the area around the Straits of Magellan near the southern tip of South America.

Habitat: Gray four-eyed frogs may live anywhere from the lowlands to mountain sites as high as 7,500 feet (2,300 meters) above sea level. Its home is in grasslands and scrubby areas, often alongside lakes.

Diet: Although they do not know for sure, scientists think these frogs eat small arthropods.

The gray four-eyed frog gets its name from the two, large, dark-colored glands on its hips. When looking at the frog from the back end, the glands look somewhat like oval-shaped eyes. (© Joseph T. Collins/Photo Researchers, Inc.)

Behavior and reproduction: Unlike many other frogs in this family, which are active mainly at night, adult gray four-eyed frogs may hop about on land both during the day and at night. They are especially active during wet weather and tend to move under stones or into cracks in or between rocks during drier spells. During the spring breeding season, males and females meet in shallow water along lakeshores. The males do not call. To mate, a male climbs onto a female's back and holds on near her hind legs. In the water, she lays a string of eggs, which hatch into grayish brown tadpoles. The tadpoles grow to as much as 1.4 inches (3.5 centimeters) long before changing into froglets.

Gray four-eyed frogs and people: People do not hunt this frog. It is not popular in the pet trade.

Conservation status: The IUCN does not consider this very common species to be endangered or threatened.   ■

Patagonia frog (*Atelognathus patagonicus*)

PATAGONIA FROG
Atelognathus patagonicus

Physical characteristics: Saggy skin is a very noticeable character-istic of the Patagonia frogs, but not all of them have it. Only the adults, which live in the water, develop the loose folds of skin on the sides of the body and on the thighs of the hind legs. The skin on younger frogs is not saggy. The upper side of the frog is tan to brown with tiny, darker brown speckles, and the underside is light orange. The head has a rather long snout that narrows toward the rounded tip, small eyes that face slightly forward, and eardrums that are hidden beneath folds of skin. The front legs are short and have unwebbed toes, while the longer hind

legs have fully webbed toes. Adults grow to 2 inches (5 centimeters) in length from the tip of the snout to the end of the rump.

Geographic range: Found only in northern Patagonia, Argentina, it lives in Laguna Blanca and small lakes in the area.

Habitat: Patagonia frogs spend most of their lives in cold, shallow, rocky-bottomed lakes, but as young frogs, they hop onto land and live under stones in tall grassy areas.

Diet: Adult Patagonia frogs eat arthropods, especially amphipods (AM-fih-pawds), that they find in the water. Amphipods are beach fleas, water lice, and other small water-living invertebrates.

Behavior and reproduction: The adult's baggy skin helps it breathe underwater. Like other frogs, the Patagonia frog can breathe through its skin. This is possible because oxygen from the water can pass right through the frog's skin and right into its blood, instead of going through the lungs first, as it does in humans. In the cold water where the Patagonia frog lives, the water has a less-than-normal amount of oxygen. With the extra folds of skin that flap in the water as the frog swims on top and between rocks on the streambed, however, the frog can take up enough oxygen to survive.

The frog's life begins when an adult female lays her small eggs on underwater plants. They hatch into golden brown tadpoles that live in the shallow water until they grow to as much as 2 inches (5 centimeters) long. They then turn into froglets that hop onto land. When they are old enough to reproduce themselves, they take to the water and develop baggy skin.

Patagonia frogs and people: People do not hunt this frog. It is not popular in the pet trade.

Conservation status: According to the World Conservation Union (IUCN), this species is Endangered, which means that it faces a very high risk of extinction in the wild. In just the 10 years between 1994 and 2004, the number of Patagonia frogs fell by half, and the largest population, which lived in a lake called Laguna Blanca, has vanished completely. Scientists blame the disappearance at Laguna Blanca on new fishes introduced into this lake. The fishes are predators of the frogs and quickly wiped out the entire population. Environmentalists fear that fishes will also be introduced into the remaining lakes and ponds where the frogs live.   ■

FOR MORE INFORMATION

Books:

Cogger, Harold G., and Richard G. Zweifel. *Encyclopedia of Reptiles and Amphibians.* San Diego, CA: Academic Press, 1998.

Halliday, Tim, and Kraig Adler, eds. *The Encyclopedia of Reptiles and Amphibians (Smithsonian Handbooks).* New York: Facts on File, 1991.

Mattison, Chris. *Frogs and Toads of the World.* New York: Facts on File Publications, 1987.

Patent, Dorothy Hinshaw. *Frogs, Toads, Salamanders, and How They Reproduce.* New York: Holiday House, 1975.

Ryan, Michael J. *The Túngara Frog.* Chicago: University of Chicago Press, 1985.

Showler, Dave. *Frogs and Toads: A Golden Guide.* New York: St. Martin's Press, 2004.

Stebbins, Robert C. *A Field Guide to Western Reptiles and Amphibians (Peterson Field Guide Series).* Boston: Houghton Mifflin, 1966.

Periodicals:

Raloff, Janet. "Hawaii's Hated Frogs: Tiny Invaders Raise a Big Ruckus." *Science News,* January 4, 2003 (vol. 163): 11.

Web sites:

"Amphibians - Leptodactylidae: Tropical Frogs." *Project Amazonas Inc.* http://www.projectamazonas.com/subpages/floraandfauna/

FloraFaunaGalleries/amphibians-tropical%20frogs%20gallery.htm (accessed on March 1, 2005).

"Atelognathus patagonicus." *CalPhotos.* http://elib.cs.berkeley.edu/ cgi/img_query?query_src=aw_lists_genera_&elarge=1111+1111+111+ 2039 (accessed on March 1, 2005).

"Big Bark, Big Bite." *American Museum of Natural History.* http://www .amnh.org/exhibitions/frogs/featured/bigbark.php (accessed on March 1, 2005).

"Ceratophrys cornuta." *Amphibians.* http://www.rieo.net/amph/exfrog/ tuno/cerato/amazon.htm (accessed on March 1, 2005).

"Family Leptodactylidae (Neotropical Frogs)." *Animal Diversity Web.* http://animaldiversity.ummz.umich.edu/site/accounts/pictures/ Leptodactylidae.html (accessed on March 1, 2005).

"Frog Legs." *American Museum of Natural History.* http://www.amnh. org/exhibitions/frogs/featured/froglegs.php (accessed on March 1, 2005).

"Lepidobatrachus laevis." *Amphibians.* http://www.rieo.net/amph/ exfrog/tuno/lepido/laevis.htm (accessed on March 1, 2005).

"Pleurodema bufonina." *CalPhotos.* http://elib.cs.berkeley.edu/ cgi/img_ query?stat=BROWSE_IMG&query_src=photos_browseimgs_amphibian_ sci&where-lifeform=Amphibian&where-taxon=Pleurodema+bufonina+ (female) (accessed on March 1, 2005).

"Smokey Jungle Frog." *Wildherps.com.* http://www.wildherps.com/ species/L.pentadactylus.html (accessed on March 1, 2005).

VOCAL SAC-BROODING FROGS

Rhinodermatidae

Class: Amphibia

Order: Anura

Family: Rhinodermatidae

Number of species: 2 species

phylum

class

subclass

order

monotypic order

suborder

▲ **family**

PHYSICAL CHARACTERISTICS

The family of vocal sac-brooding frogs has only two species: Darwin's frog and Chile Darwin's frog. Both of these little frogs have flattened heads that come to a fleshy point at the tip of the snout. With their large eyes and thin, nearly beak-shaped snout, these frogs almost have a bird-like face. The pointy snout tip is especially noticeable because it comes at the end of two ridges, one found on each side of the body and extending from nearly the rump all the way to the snout. Another fainter ridge runs along the upper lip to the bottom of each large, gold-colored eye and down each front leg. The front legs are shorter than the hind legs, but all four are slender. The toes on the front feet have no webbing, but most if not all of the hind toes are at least partially webbed. Both species have a bump, or tubercle (TOO-ber-kul), on each hind foot. Their bodies may be light brown, reddish brown, brown, light green, or dark green, sometimes with brown, gray, or green markings. At least part of the underside, usually including the hind legs and lower part of the belly, is black with large white spots or blotches.

Although the two species look much alike, they are slightly different. The Chile Darwin's frog has webbing between all of the toes on its hind feet, while the Darwin's frog does not have any webbing between its outer two hind toes. In addition, the tubercles on the hind feet of the Chile Darwin's frog are larger than those on the Darwin's frog.

The two members of this family are small frogs. A male Darwin's frog grows to 0.9 to 1.1 inches (2.2 to 2.8 centimeters), and the female reaches 1 to 1.2 inches (2.5 to 3.1 centimeters). The Chile Darwin's frog is slightly larger. The male grows to 1.2 inches (3.1 centimeters), and the female reaches 1.3 inches (3.3 centimeters) in length. The males and females of both species look much alike except during the breeding season when the male's chest may be puffed up with eggs or tadpoles.

GEOGRAPHIC RANGE

As its name suggests, Chile Darwin's frog lives in Chile. In particular, its home is in the central part of the country in areas between about 160 and 1,640 feet (50 to 500 meters) above sea level. Darwin's frog lives in the same area as Chile Darwin's frog and also farther south through Chile and into far western Argentina. They can be found from sea level to about 4,900 feet (1,500 meters) above sea level.

HABITAT

These frogs live in wet forests where beech trees grow and sometimes in open fields near houses and buildings. They usually do not wander too far from either wetlands or lazy streams.

DIET

Scientists do not know for sure, but they think these two species eat whatever insects and other invertebrates they can find.

BEHAVIOR AND REPRODUCTION

Mostly active during the day, the vocal sac-brooding frogs likely find a spot in the forest or field and settle in to wait for an insect or other small invertebrate to wander by. The frogs then quickly nab the passing meal. The two species are active most of the year, but disappear in cold, winter months. The frogs probably wait for warmer weather from a sheltered spot under a layer of moss or a rotting log, but scientists do not

DIFFERENT CALL, DIFFERENT SPECIES

Until scientists took a closer look, they thought Darwin's frog was the only member of the vocal sac-brooding family. One of the clues they used to decide that the frogs were actually two different species instead of one was that some males were making one type of call and others were making a different-sounding call. The call is very important among frogs because females use it to find males who are ready to mate. If a male's call is different—even if he looks just like every other male frog in the forest—a female will not answer his call and will not mate with him. An important requirement for animals to be of the same species is that the males and females must recognize each other as possible mating partners.

know for sure where the frogs go in the winter. When the Darwin's frog is threatened, it flips onto its back and lies still. This display shows off the frog's bright black-and-white pattern, which may scare off a predator. The Chile Darwin's frog, which also has the black-and-white underside, probably does the same thing.

Once spring comes, the frogs again appear in the woods and meadows. Each male performs his nighttime calls from land and draws in a female. Darwin's frog calls quickly repeat a "pi-i-i-i-ip" over and over again. The male Chile Darwin's frog sings a fast "pip-pip-pip-pip" and waits a few seconds before repeating the short call. In both species, the female lays her eggs on the ground and leaves the parenting job to the male. A female Chile Darwin frog lays one or two dozen small eggs, while a female Darwin's frog lays three to seven larger eggs. The male in both species stays with the eggs until they are almost ready to hatch, then scoops them up with his mouth. The eggs slide back into his vocal sac, a balloon-like structure in the areas of his throat and chest that inflates and deflates when he calls. Since he has already mated and no longer needs to use the vocal sac to call in females, it provides a safe spot for the eggs to hatch into tadpoles. In about eight days, the male Chile Darwin's frog hops over to a stream or pool, and the young tadpoles squirm out of his vocal sac and into the water, where they later turn into froglets. In Darwin's frog, the tadpoles remain in the male's vocal sac for 50 to 70 days until they turn into froglets. Only then do they crawl outside.

VOCAL SAC-BROODING FROGS AND PEOPLE

People do not hunt and eat these frogs, and they do not commonly see them in the pet trade. Scientists are interested in the frogs because of the unusual role of the male in the development of his young.

CONSERVATION STATUS

According to the World Conservation Union (IUCN), Chile Darwin's frog is Critically Endangered, which means that it faces an extremely high risk of extinction in the wild; and Darwin's frog is Vulnerable, which means that it faces a high risk of extinction in the wild.

The Chile Darwin's frog is especially at risk. Since 1994, at least 80 percent of all members of this species have disappeared, and some scientists fear that it may already be extinct. People had seen Chile Darwin's frogs in their habitat until 1978, but trips to find the frog since then have found nothing. Scientists are not sure why this frog has vanished, but think that habitat loss, and particularly the removal of the plants where they live, may be part of the reason.

Darwin's frog (*Rhinoderma darwinii*)

DARWIN'S FROG
Rhinoderma darwinii

Physical characteristics: Darwin's frog, which is also sometimes called Darwin's toad, is a pudgy frog with a triangle-shaped head that ends in a very pointy snout. A ridge runs down each side of the body from the snout over the eye and almost to the rump. Its gold-colored eyes are on the sides of its head. No eardrums show. Its back, the top of its head, and the top of its legs are light brown with gray blotches. The underside of the frog is often light to dark brown on the throat and chest, and black with white blotches toward the belly and on the back legs. The toes on the front feet are unwebbed, but most of the toes on the hind feet have at least some

The male Darwin's frog stays with his eggs until they are almost ready to hatch, then scoops them up with his mouth. The eggs slide back into his vocal sac. Since he no longer needs to use the vocal sac to call in females, it provides a safe spot for the eggs to hatch into tadpoles. (Illustration by Wendy Baker. Reproduced by permission.)

webbing. The space between the two outer toes on the hind feet has no webbing. The frog also has a small bump, or tubercle, on its hind foot.

Females are slightly larger than males and can grow to 1 to 1.2 inches (2.5 to 3.1 centimeters) long from snout to rump. Males usually reach 0.9 to 1.1 inches (2.2 to 2.8 centimeters) in length. Besides their size, males and females look alike except during the mating season, when the male's chest may be puffed out because of its unusual breeding behavior.

Geographic range: Darwin's frog lives in central and southern Chile and continues across the border into far western Argentina.

Habitat: Darwin's frogs live in beech-tree forests and in fields, sometimes in areas near houses and buildings. They also live near and often in slow streams and swamps.

Diet: Ambush hunters, they sit still and wait for an insect or other small invertebrate to wander by closely enough to grab and eat it.

Behavior and reproduction: Darwin's frogs are active during the daytime, and they spend a considerable amount of time sunbathing, or basking. Although their body shape and color allow them to avoid notice much of the time, predators do sometimes discover this little frog. When the attacker approaches, the frog defends itself by throwing itself onto its back and playing dead. If the frog is near water, it jumps in first, then flips over and floats downstream while lying upside down. Both displays show off the frog's black and white underside and may frighten off a predator.

The most unusual behavior in this frog, however, is in its reproduction. Their breeding season begins in spring and continues into summer. In the daytime and occasionally at night during this time, each male makes his call, quickly repeating "pi-i-i-i-ip" over and over again. When he calls, he draws air into a vocal sac on his throat, which inflates and deflates like a balloon. When the female responds, he leads her to his nest, which is a hidden spot on land. She then squirms under his body, so that he winds up on top of her back. Instead of holding on to her back very tightly as other frogs do, the male Darwin's frog barely clasps her. She lays about three to seven eggs and leaves the male to take care of them for about 20 days when they are almost ready to hatch. He then gobbles them up. The eggs drop into his vocal sac, hatch there into tadpoles, and remain inside for another 50 to 70 days until they turn into froglets. During this time, the male's chest is puffed large with developing tadpoles. Scientists think the tadpoles survive by slowly eating the leftover yolk from their eggs, as well as some food provided by the male's body through the skin lining his vocal sac. The new froglets crawl out of the vocal sac, through their father's mouth, and to the outside, where they begin hopping about on land.

Darwin's frogs and people: Scientists are interested in this frog because of the unusual way that the male is involved in reproduction.

Conservation status: According to the IUCN, Darwin's frog is Vulnerable, which means that it faces a high risk of extinction in the wild. According to scientists who have studied the frog, it is now much less common than it was in the 1980s and 1990s, and it has vanished completely from some areas, including places inside national parks and other preserves. They believe a main reason for the frogs' disappearance in unprotected places is the loss of their habitat, especially due to logging of the forests where they live. In addition, the climate is becoming drier in this part of the world and may be making it harder for the frogs to survive. ∎

FOR MORE INFORMATION

Books:

Halliday, Tim, and Kraig Adler, eds. *The Encyclopedia of Reptiles and Amphibians (Smithsonian Handbooks)*. New York: Facts on File, 1991.

Mattison, Chris. *Frogs and Toads of the World*. New York: Facts on File Publications, 1987.

Miller, Sara Swan. *Frogs and Toads: The Leggy Leapers*. New York: Franklin Watts, 2000.

Patent, Dorothy Hinshaw. *Frogs, Toads, Salamanders, and How They Reproduce*. New York: Holiday House, 1975.

Showler, Dave. *Frogs and Toads: A Golden Guide*. New York: St. Martin's Press, 2004.

Web sites:

Churchman, Deborah. "Hoppy Birthdays - Frogs." *Ranger Rick*. http://www.findarticles.com/p/articles/mi_m0EPG/is_4_36/ai_90445325 (accessed on March 10, 2005).

"Dads at Work." *Time for Kids Classroom*. http://www.timeforkids.com/TFK/class/ns/article/0,17585,490974,00.html (accessed on March 10, 2005).

"Strange Breeding: Darwin's Frog." *Frogland*. http://allaboutfrogs.org/weird/strange/darwins.html (accessed on March 10, 2005).

family

PHYSICAL CHARACTERISTICS

This family includes some of the smallest frogs in the world. Depending on the species, adults grow to just 0.3 to 0.8 inches (0.8 to 2 centimeters) long from the tip of the short, rounded snout to the end of the rump. Although the frogs are small, they have somewhat chunky, strong-looking bodies. Their front legs are thin and end in two, sometimes three, stubby toes. They have the bones for the other two toes under their skin, but these toes do not show. Their hind legs likewise show only three, sometimes four, very short toes. Each toe bone in the four feet is shaped like a "T" at the tip. The skeleton is also a bit odd in these frogs because it has no middle chest bone, or sternum, but does have a covering of bone across the front of the chest. Most species also have bony plates, or shields, under the skin of the back. The shield attaches to the backbone. Because of this shield, the three-toed toadlets are sometimes called saddlebacks. The southern three-toed toadlet does not have the shield.

Several of the frogs in this family, including the southern three-toed toadlet and some of the pumpkin toadlets, are bright orange. The pumpkin toadlet is sometimes yellow instead. The southern three-toed toadlet has black patches along its sides, parts of its legs, and around its eyes. Other frogs in this family are shades of brown and blend into the background a bit better.

Scientists either group all six species into one genus, called *Brachycephalus* or put two of the species in their own genus, named *Psyllophryne*. As of 2002, many scientists now use only *Brachycephalus* because they think all six species are very closely related. At one time, scientists thought that the three-toed toadlets should be part of the "true toad" family, named Bufonidae. When they took a closer look, however, they found that the toadlets were missing an organ that the true toads have. It is called Bidder's organ and is a small growth of female-type tissue on part of the male's reproductive system.

GEOGRAPHIC RANGE

All six species live in different areas within the far eastern part of central and southern Brazil along the Atlantic Ocean coastline.

HABITAT

The tiny frogs in this family live among the leaves that cover the ground of warm, humid forests. They often live in forests on mountainsides up to 2,240 feet (750 meters) above sea level. They also breed on land.

DIET

Members of this family eat various arthropods (AR-thro-pawds). Arthropods are animals without backbones, or invertebrates (in-VER-teh-brehts), that have jointed legs. The diets of most three-toed toadlets include mites and springtails. Mites are small, spider-like arthropods. Springtails (sometimes called snow fleas in colder climates) are a type of very tiny insect that has a little clip on its underside. When the insect quickly unfastens its clip, the creature springs through the air. Three-toed toadlets find mites, springtails, and other small invertebrates in the leaves that are scattered on the ground.

BEHAVIOR AND REPRODUCTION

In the dry season of the year, these frogs find shelter under logs or beneath piles of leaves on the ground. They become active when the rainy season comes and wander about on land during the daytime. They typically walk rather than hop, using their thin front legs and longer hind legs to crawl among leaves on the forest floor. The males set up and defend territories against other males. A male calls to keep intruding males away, but if that does not work, he may begin wrestling with the other male and try to push him out of the area.

Scientists have not done careful studies of all six species, but they think that they probably all reproduce in the same general way. In the breeding period, which also takes place during

WHEN IS A TOADLET NOT A TOAD?

The three-toed toadlets of South America have a confusing name, because they are not actually toads at all. Scientists group all true toads into a single family, named Bufonidae. Young toads in this family are called toadlets. None of the other species of frogs are true toads, even if they have warty skin and look very much like toads. People who are not scientists, however, often are the ones who give frogs their common names, and they sometimes name warty-looking frogs "toads." The three-toed toadlets are an example. People called them toadlets because they look toad-y and they are small. Three-toed toadlets, however, are not part of the family Bufonidae and, scientifically speaking, are not really toads or toadlets at all.

the rainy season, the males call from their territories on land. The call of the pumpkin toadlet and the southern three-toed toadlet is a buzzy sound. The females hear the calls and approach the males. When a female comes close, a male will climb onto her back and use his front legs to hold onto her in front of her hind legs. The male frog, at least among the pumpkin toadlets, then scoots forward until he is hanging onto her body near her front legs. This type of piggyback grasp is called amplexus (am-PLEK-sus). Once the male is in the right position, the female lays her eggs, which are quite big compared to the size of the frog. She lays them on leaves or sometimes under a log. Because her eggs are so large, the female only has a few eggs. A female pumpkin toadlet, for example, lays five or fewer eggs, each of them 0.2 inches (5.1 to 5.3 millimeters) in diameter. The toadlet that is known by its scientific name *Brachycephalus didactyla* lays only one egg per clutch. Instead of hatching into tadpoles as happens in many other species of frogs, three-toed toadlet eggs hatch directly into baby toadlets, sometimes with a tiny bit of tail that disappears shortly. Pumpkin toadlets hatch 64 days after the female laid the eggs.

THREE-TOED TOADLETS AND PEOPLE

Scientists are studying the pumpkin toadlet because its skin oozes a poison that might be useful in making some medicines.

CONSERVATION STATUS

The World Conservation Union (IUCN) lists three species of three-toed toadlets as Data Deficient, which means too little information is available to make a judgment about the threat of extinction. The three species are *Brachycephalus nodoterga*, which is sometimes called a saddleback toad, *Brachycephalus pernix*, and *Brachycephalus vertebralis*.

Brachycephalus nodoterga lives in a very small area. In fact, it has only been found in one place: in forests that have never been cut down and about 3,280 feet (1,000 meters) above sea level. More studies will help scientists learn details about this frog's life and what specific type of habitat and other things it needs to continue to survive in the wild. *Brachycephalus pernix* also lives in a small area. This species makes its home in mountain forests about 1,475 feet (450 meters) above sea level. Although its entire habitat is inside a protected area, conservationists fear that too many tourists in the forests may be trampling over the leaf-covered ground and accidentally harming the frogs that live there. *Brachycephalus vertebralis* is the third species listed by the IUCN as Data Deficient. This small frog also lives in the mountain forests of southern Brazil along the coast of the Atlantic Ocean. Its home is about 2,625 feet (800 meters) above sea level. First discovered in the late 1990s, it has not been seen since despite repeated searches. Destruction of the forests in southern Brazil may harm the toadlet, as well as the other two Data Deficient species in this family.

Pumpkin toadlet (*Brachycephalus ephippium*)

PUMPKIN TOADLET
Brachycephalus ephippium

Physical characteristics: Reaching just 0.5 to 0.8 inches (1.25 to 2 centimeters) long, the pumpkin toadlet is one of the smallest frogs on the planet. Its name comes from its bright orange color, its warty skin, and its tiny size. Sometimes the frog's color is yellow rather than orange, and people call it a gold frog instead. Its head has a short, rounded snout and two large, black eyes. Beneath the skin of its back, this toadlet has a bony plate or shield that is attached to the backbone. The bony plate led to the third common name of this species, Spix's saddleback toad. Its front legs are thin and end in two, stubby

toes. The slender hind legs, which are longer than the front pair, end in three stubby toes. The other toes on their feet are either just nubs or missing altogether. The bones inside the toes are each shaped like a "T" at the tip.

Geographic range: Pumpkin toadlets live in southeastern Brazil along the Atlantic coast.

Habitat: These frogs live and breed in humid, warm forests along the ocean. They spend most of their time in piles of dead leaves that cover the ground.

Diet: Pumpkin toadlets scrounge around in the leaf piles for small arthropods, including mites and tiny insects called springtails. Studies of pumpkin toadlets show that the frogs get more than half of their diet from springtails.

Behavior and reproduction: Pumpkin toadlets, which are active during the daytime in the rainy season, are not difficult to spot. Their bright orange or yellow color is very noticeable as these tiny frogs slowly walk over leaves. If the day is very humid, they may climb onto low branches of bushes and trees. In a rather unusual behavior, this frog swipes its front and back legs over its head on down its body. The frog performs this leg-waving movement when cleaning its body of dirt. A male frog also will wave its front legs in front of its eyes when another male comes close. This sometimes scares off the newcomer. If it does not work, the

Reaching just 0.5 to 0.8 inches (1.25 to 2 centimeters) long, the pumpkin toadlet is one of the smallest frogs on the planet. Its name comes from its bright orange color, its warty skin, and its tiny size. Sometimes the frog's color is yellow rather than orange, and people call it a gold frog instead. (Photograph by B. Kevin Schafer/Corbis.)

male will protect his territory by wrestling with and shoving the other male until he leaves.

Each male calls from his own territory during the rainy season. He holds his body up high, draws in air to fill up his vocal sac, and performs his call, which is a repeated buzzing sound. When a female approaches, he wraps his front legs around her waist and then walks with her in this position as she shuffles around looking for a good spot to lay her eggs. Once she finds a site under a log or in a pile of leaves, the male scoots up to grab onto her near her front legs. For the next 30 minutes or so, she lays her eggs. Females usually lay five, large, yellowish white eggs at a time. After the female lays the eggs, the male leaves, but the female stays behind for a few moments to roll the eggs along the ground with her hind feet. Now covered with dirt, the eggs are well-hidden from the view of predators. The eggs hatch 64 days later, skipping the tadpole stage, and small, reddish brown toadlets crawl out. The newborn toadlets have a tiny tail, but this disappears soon.

Pumpkin toadlets and people: Scientists are studying the medical uses of the very strong poisons, or toxins, that ooze from this frog's skin. The toxins affect the heart and other muscles and the nerves.

Conservation status: The IUCN does not consider this frog to be at risk. Although it lives in a fairly small area, the pumpkin toadlet is quite common there. In addition, part of its habitat falls within various protected areas. ∎

FOR MORE INFORMATION

Books:

Mattison, Chris. *Frogs and Toads of the World.* New York: Facts on File Publications, 1987.

Showler, Dave. *Frogs and Toads: A Golden Guide.* New York: St. Martin's Press, 2004.

Web sites:

"Brachycephalidae." *AmphibiaWeb.* http://elib.cs.berkeley.edu/aw/lists/Brachycephalidae.shtml (accessed on March 8, 2005).

"*Brachycephalus pernix.*" *AmphibiaWeb.* http://elib.cs.berkeley.edu/cgi-bin/amphib_query?query_src=aw_lists_genera_&where-genus=Brachycephalus&where-species=pernix (accessed on March 8, 2005).

Cannatella, David. "Brachycephalidae." *Texas Memorial Museum, University of Texas, Austin.* http://www.zo.utexas.edu/research/

salientia/brachycephalidae/brachycephalidae.html (accessed on March 8, 2005).

"Psyllophryne hermogenesi." AmphibiaWeb. http://elib.cs.berkeley.edu/cgi-bin/amphib_query?query_src=aw_lists_genera_&where-genus=Psyllophryne&where-species=hermogenesi (accessed on March 8, 2005).

Watson, Eduardo Cörner. "Little Frog." http://www.grindelwald.com.br/sapo/ (accessed on March 8, 2005).

family

CHAPTER

PHYSICAL CHARACTERISTICS

The toads in this family are known as the "true" toads. All other frogs that are called toads are not really toads. They may have a toad's body shape or have numerous warts, but they are not true toads. One of the features true toads have that no other type of frog has is a Bidder's organ. A Bidder's organ is a female body part that is found inside a male toad. This organ does not appear to do anything in a healthy male toad. It does, however, help to tell a true toad apart from all other species of frogs that exist on Earth.

True toads have other hidden features, too. They have an odd joint between their lower backbone, or spine, and their hip bones that makes it difficult for the toads to jump well. They can walk or hop short distances, but they cannot leap several feet like some of the other species of frogs. They have only seven bones in their spines instead of the eight that most other frogs have; they have fewer bones in their front and back feet, and they have shorter toes than other frogs typically have. In addition, the pair of shoulder blades, which are usually separate in other frogs, are fused together in toads into one big shoulder blade that stretches across the whole upper back. Their lack of teeth also sets the true toads apart. None of the true toads have teeth on the upper jaw, while almost all other frogs do.

The most noticeable feature of true toads is their warty skin, especially the huge "wart" on the back of the head. The big "wart" is called a paratoid (pair-RAH-toyd) gland and makes a white, liquid poison that looks like milk. Not all true toads have paratoid glands, but the glands are usually very noticeable in the toads that do have them. The pair of paratoid glands on the American toad, for example, looks like large, flat water balloons that extend from behind the eye to the front of the back. Some species of frogs that are not true toads also have paratoid glands, so just seeing a paratoid gland is not enough to identify a frog as a true toad.

Many toads have plump bodies, short heads with rounded snouts and large mouths, eardrums that are visible on the sides of the head, short legs, and numerous warts on their backs and legs. The Houston toad is a good example. It has a fat-looking, round body that is covered with many small warts. Its head is short with a wide mouth and visible eardrums. Its front legs are thick but rather short, and its hind legs are much shorter than the legs of a leaping frog. Some of the toads in this family, however, look little like this typical toad. The harlequin frog, which is actually one of the true toads, has long and thin front legs, long hind legs, a thin body, no eardrums, and quite smooth skin.

In general, true toads are shades of brown, green, and/or gray, which allows these rather slow creatures to blend in with the background. The Chirinda toad, for instance, has a light brown back and legs and dark brown sides. When it sits still, it almost disappears against the dead leaves of its habitat. The green toad, which lives in Europe, Asia, and northern Africa, is brown with green blotches, a pattern that blends in with the ground where it lives. A few species, however, have very bright colors. The Yungas redbelly toad has a black and sometimes green back, but a bright red belly, and the male golden toad, which is now extinct, or no longer in existence, was vivid orange.

True toads also come in many different sizes. The Roraima bush toad, which lives in South America, grows to only 0.8 inches (2 centimeters) long from the tip of the snout to the end of the rump, while the marine toad can reach 9 inches (23 centimeters) in length. The Rococo or Cururu toad, can grow even larger, sometimes reaching nearly 10 inches (25.4 centimeters) long.

GEOGRAPHIC RANGE

Members of this family live throughout much of the world, including all continents except Antarctica. They do not naturally live in Australia, but people have introduced them there, and the toads are doing well.

HABITAT

True toads, harlequin frogs, and their relatives make their homes for most of the year in a variety of habitats from wet or dry forests to fields, and even some dry deserts. They can survive in very warm, tropical areas, as well as cooler places with snowy winter seasons. They do not live in far northern North America or northern Asia, but some exist without problem high on windswept or snow-capped mountains that are up to 16,400 feet (5,000 meters) above sea level. The vast majority of toads are terrestrial (te-REH-stree-uhl), which means they live on land. Examples of terrestrial toads include the American toad, the marine toad, and the Houston toad.

Only a few true toads climb and live in trees or spend most of their time in the water. One of the toads that is arboreal (ar-BOR-ee-ul), which means that it lives in trees, is the brown tree toad of Borneo, Sumatra, Malaysia, and Thailand, which are all in southeastern Asia. Using the wide pads on the tips of its toes to help it cling to twigs and branches, this toad usually stays in the trees except during mating season, when it enters streams. The aquatic swamp toad, on the other hand, is aquatic (uh-QUOT-ik), which means that it usually remains in the water. This large toad, which also lives in parts of southeastern Asia, has full webbing between its toes to help it swim.

DIET

Most toads eat insects, spiders, and other arthropods (AR-throepawds). Arthropods are animals that do not have backbones, but have jointed legs. Those that live in rainforests eat quite a few ants, which are plentiful there. Some, like the American toad, will also eat an occasional earthworm. The larger species, including the marine toads, eat a great many insects, but they can and sometimes do eat larger animals, including mice, other frogs, and lizards.

BEHAVIOR AND REPRODUCTION

Many true toads are mainly active at night, when they come out of hiding to hunt for food. One of these, the Colorado river toad, lives in the deserts of the western United States. It avoids the hot daytime sun by staying underground and comes out at night to search the sand for beetles, snails, and other invertebrates (in-VER-teh-brehts). Invertebrates are arthropods and other animals without backbones. A few toads, including the Yungas redbelly toad, are active during the day.

Like most other frogs, toads have small poison glands in their skin. In many toads, some of the poison glands group together to form the paratoid glands, one of which is located behind each eye. When the toad feels threatened, it can ooze and sometimes squirt the milky poison from these glands. To some predators the poison tastes bad, but it can make others sick or even cause them to die if they swallow enough. Some toads, like the harlequin frog, do not have paratoid glands, but still are able to ooze enough poison through their other skin glands to ward off predators. This is an important defense tactic in the toads, many of which can only hop short distances and often cannot escape a predator by running away. Some toads, like the American toad, will even turn to face a predator, which puts the paratoid glands in the attacker's face. Not all predators are bothered by a toad's poison. The hog-nosed snake, for instance, makes toads a regular part of its diet.

Some toads, like the Yungas redbelly toad, do something different when they feel threatened. They strike a stiff pose, called the unken (OONK-en) reflex. In this position, they arch the back while holding up their red-bottomed feet and showing off the red of the belly. This display and the flash of color probably helps to remind predators that the toads have poisonous skin.

Many true toads mate during wet times of the year, often in the spring rainy season. In many species, a heavy rain will bring hundreds of males to ponds, streams, or newly filled pools of water where they begin calling. Toads often mate in the small pools that are only filled with water part of the year. These pools do not contain fish, which might eat the toads and/or their young. The typical male true toad has a balloonlike bit of flesh on its throat that inflates and deflates. This flesh, called a vocal sac, allows the toad to call. The males of most other types of frogs also have vocal sacs. Most of the true toads call with a steady trill. The American toad, for example, has a beautiful, long trill that lasts several seconds. Others, like the brown tree toad, have voices that are more like squawks than trills.

True toads usually call in choruses, which means that the males of a species group together and call all at once. The females hear the calls and follow them to the males. They mate when the male grasps the female from behind and holds on near her front legs, while the female lays her eggs in the water. In some species, like the Houston toad, the male may have to cling to the female's back for several hours before the female

is ready to lay her eggs. Malcolm's Ethiopian toad mates differently than other true toads. Instead of the piggyback position that other toads and the vast majority of frogs use, the male and female of this species mate belly to belly.

Usually, the female lays her eggs, often hundreds of them, in a long string. The egg string may wrap around underwater plants, but sometimes it simply floats in the water. Most toads leave their eggs after they are laid. Toad eggs commonly hatch in a week or two into tiny tadpoles. American toad tadpoles, including their tails, are often no longer than a person's fingernail. The tadpole stage is also quite short, and they can turn into toadlets in just a few weeks. The toadlets are typically very small. People walking through the forest are frequently surprised at toadlets' tiny size. Baby American toads are also no bigger than a fingernail. Even the enormous marine toad has small toadlets.

A few toads, like the Roraima bush toad, probably have eggs that turn into toadlets instead of changing into tadpoles first. Scientists are not sure about the bush toad, however, because they have never watched an egg hatch.

TRUE TOADS, HARLEQUIN FROGS, THEIR RELATIVES, AND PEOPLE

People have been interested in toads for many, many years, and they have written about toads in many, many books, especially make-believe children's books. Children find living toads interesting, in part because usually the toads are quite simple to catch. People should, however, be careful not to put their hands into their mouths after touching a toad until they have washed their hands. This is good practice after handling any animal. Toads are not hunted for food, but some toads are common in the pet trade.

CONSERVATION STATUS

The World Conservation Union (IUCN) lists five species in this family as Extinct, which means that they are no longer in existence. These include the golden toad, the last of which was seen in 1989; the jambato toad, last seen in 1988; the longnose stub-foot toad, last seen in 1989; and two other species known only by their scientific names: *Adenomus kandianus*, last seen more than one hundred years ago; and *Atelopus vogli*, the only individuals of which were seen only during a 1933 expedition and in just one spot in the world. Scientists are especially concerned about the species that disappeared in the late 1980s. Although they are not certain, they believe that the frogs may have died off because of infection with a fungus, known as chytrid (KIT-rid) fungus, which has harmed many different species around the world. Global warming, which has changed the world's weather patterns, pollution, the introduction of fish that eat frogs, and loss of habitat may also have played a role in some of the species' extinctions.

ROCK AND ROLL

The Roraima bush toad defends itself from predators in a bizarre way. The toad, which grows to barely 0.8 inches long (2 centimeters), cannot leap or even take small hops. Instead, it slowly walks over the rocks in its habitat. When it feels threatened, this toad tucks itself into a little ball and rolls down the side of the rock, giving it the look of just another tiny stone falling away.

In addition, the IUCN lists the Wyoming toad as Extinct in the wild. This means that the frog is no longer alive except in captivity or through the aid of humans. The Wyoming has a typical toad appearance: chubby body, numerous warts on its back and legs, large paratoid glands, and a short, round-snouted face. It once lived in a larger part of Wyoming and was quite common in the 1950s, but began to disappear in the 1960s. Scientists had thought that it had already become extinct by the 1980s, but a small population turned up in 1987. The toad now only exists within a national wildlife refuge. Currently, ecologists are keeping a watchful eye on the population and are raising toadlets in captivity to release into the refuge. Without this help, scientists believe the toads would likely have already become extinct. They are unsure why the frogs are disappearing, but think that the chytrid fungus may have been a cause.

Other frogs noted by the IUCN include eighty-two species that are Critically Endangered and face an extremely high risk of extinction in the wild; seventy species that are Endangered and face a very high risk of extinction in the wild; forty-nine that are Vulnerable and face a high risk of extinction in the wild; twenty-six that are Near Threatened and at risk of becoming threatened with extinction in the future; and sixty that are Data Deficient, which means that scientists do not have enough information to make a judgment about the threat of extinction.

The U.S. Fish and Wildlife Service lists three U.S. species as being Endangered and one as Threatened. The Endangered species are the Wyoming toad, which was described above, the Houston toad, and the arroyo or southwestern toad. The Threatened species is the Puerto Rican crested toad.

The Houston toad, which the IUCN also considers to be Endangered, once lived in Texas along the coast of the Gulf of Mexico. It became less common in the last half of the twentieth century when the city of Houston became bigger and people began building in what had been the toad's habitat. In addition, the area had a spell of extremely dry weather, which also hurt the toads. The toads now live in a much smaller area.

Half of the arroyo toads, listed by both the U.S. Fish and Wildlife Service and the IUCN as Threatened, disappeared between 1994 and 2004. The toads make their homes in parts of northwestern Mexico and California. The drop in their numbers probably happened as the result of several things, including the construction of roads, dams, and buildings; too much cattle grazing, which is hurting the plants in the frog's habitat, and the introduction of frog-eating fish to the toads' habitat.

Only twenty percent of the Puerto Rican crested toads that lived on Earth in 1994 were left by 2004. As of 2004, fewer than 250 adult toads remained in the wild. The species is listed as Threatened by the U.S. Fish and Wildlife Service and Critically Endangered by the IUCN. The toad, which is native to Puerto Rico and the British Virgin Islands, probably disappeared because people began cutting down and building in the forest where the toads lived so people could move into and live in the area. According to the IUCN, people drained the pools of water where the toads once mated and laid their eggs to make the area into parking lots. Scientists have been able to raise baby crested toads in captivity, but when they are set free, these young toads die. One small population of toads still survives in the wild. It lives inside a national forest and appears to be safe from further habitat destruction.

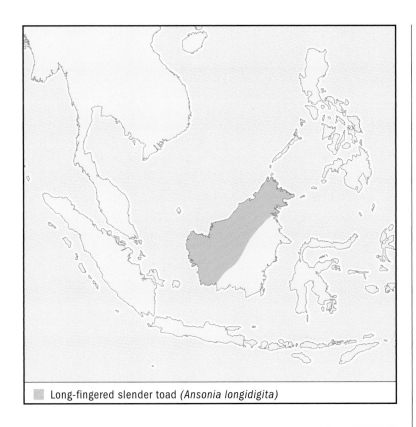

Long-fingered slender toad (*Ansonia longidigita*)

LONG-FINGERED SLENDER TOAD
Ansonia longidigita

Physical characteristics: Also known as the long-fingered stream toad, the long-fingered slender toad has very long and thin front and back legs. Its front legs are about as long as its body. The front legs and back legs also have very long, thin toes. The toad's body is rather slender, and its back is covered with small warts. It has a small head, but it has large, brown eyes and a large mouth. The snout hangs a bit beyond the lower jaw, making the frog look as if it has a slight overbite.

Unlike many other toads, it does not have the large poison "warts," called paratoid glands, behind its head. The frog is dark brown to reddish brown, sometimes with faded black bands noticeable on its hind legs. Males and females look similar, but the females are a bit bigger. Males typically grow to 1.4 to 2 inches (3.5 to 5 centimeters) long from snout to rump, while females usually reach about 1.8 to 2.8 inches (4.5 to 7 centimeters) in length.

Geographic range: The long-fingered slender toad is native to Borneo.

Habitat: The long-fingered slender toad lives among forests from the bottoms of mountains up to about 7,220 feet (2,200 meters). It breeds near fast-flowing streams and in steep places.

Diet: Adults eat small insects, especially ants, of the rainforest. Tadpoles eat plants that they find growing on rocks in the streams where they live.

Behavior and reproduction: Scientists know little about the behavior of these toads outside of their mating time. To breed, males group together next to rocky streams and call females with high-pitched trills. Eggs hatch into tadpoles, which have a sucking mouth on the underside. This helps the tadpole hang onto plants or rocks in the fast water of the stream in which they live until they change into toadlets.

Long-fingered slender toads and people: People very rarely see this toad in the wild, and scientists know little about it.

Conservation status: The World Conservation Union (IUCN) has listed this toad as Near Threatened, which means that it is at risk of becoming threatened with extinction in the future. It lives in areas around streams, and these areas are changing as the forests are cut.

Logging not only removes trees, but allows soil to flow into the streams, muddying them and making them unsuitable for the tadpoles. Scientists fear that the number of frogs will soon drop as their habitat is destroyed. Fortunately, some populations of this species live in areas where logging is not allowed. ■

Harlequin frog (*Atelopus varius*)

HARLEQUIN FROG
Atelopus varius

Physical characteristics: Also known as the harlequin toad, the harlequin frog may come in several different colors, always with a bright pattern of blotches on a dark, usually black, background. The bright pattern is often yellow, but may also be another color like green, orange, or red. The frog gets its common name from these colors. A harlequin is a court jester, a person who hundreds of years ago wore gaudy, colorful costumes to entertain an audience.

The frog has very thin but long front legs. Its back legs are a bit thicker and still longer. Its eardrum is not visible. Males grow to about 1.1 to 1.6 inches (2.7 to 4 centimeters) long from snout to rump. The females are larger, reaching 1.3 to 1.9 inches (3.4 to 4.8 centimeters) in length. In some populations, the females and males look much alike, but in others, the males and females come in different colors.

Geographic range: Harlequin frogs live in Costa Rica and Panama in far southern Central America.

Habitat: Harlequin frogs live in moist forests in valleys and partway up the sides of mountains. Scientists have not seen the frogs mating in the wild, but they believe these frogs do so in rocky streams, because this is where they have found harlequin frog tadpoles.

Diet: They eat small arthropods, including spiders and insects, like caterpillars, flies, and ants.

Behavior and reproduction: At night, harlequin frogs sleep on top of large leaves above streams. They are active during the day, hopping about in plain view. Their bright colors help remind predators that the frogs can ooze a very poisonous and bad-tasting liquid from their skin. The poison in the liquid is the same as that found in the very dangerous puffer fish. Males set up territories and make short buzzing sounds to tell other males to stay away. Sometimes, the males will fight by jumping on or chasing one another. They may also circle a front foot in the air before or after a fight. Unlike the males of other frogs, harlequin frog males do not call females for breeding. They do, however, mate like most other frogs with males climbing onto the backs of females. A harlequin frog female may carry a male on her back for several days until she has finished laying her eggs.

Harlequin frogs and people: Humans almost never see this extremely rare frog.

Conservation status: The World Conservation Union (IUCN) has listed this frog as Critically Endangered and facing an extremely high risk of extinction in the wild, because most of them have disappeared since 1988. In 1996, in fact, scientists feared that all of the more than one hundred populations known to exist in Costa Rica were already gone. Seven years later, however, a tiny population was discovered there. Some populations still live in Panama, but their numbers appear to be dropping. Scientists believe that the frogs are mainly disappearing because of infection with a fungus, called chytrid fungus, which is also killing many other frogs worldwide. In addition, people have introduced trout, a popular game fish, to some of the waterways in which the frogs breed. The trout eat harlequin frogs. ■

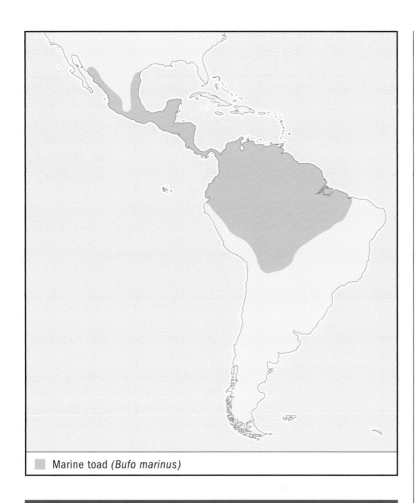

Marine toad *(Bufo marinus)*

MARINE TOAD
Bufo marinus

Physical characteristics: The marine toad is an enormous toad that can grow to as much as 9 inches (23 centimeters) long from snout to rump and weigh up to 2.2 pounds (1.5 kilograms). Sometimes it is called the giant toad, and in Belize, its nickname is the spring chicken. It is a dark-colored toad, often gray to brown, and sometimes reddish brown. Frequently, it has darker brown blotches and sometimes white spots on its back. It has large paratoid glands spreading from the back of its head to the front legs. It has a short, rounded snout, large eyes, and a noticeable eardrum on each side of its head.

The marine toad is an enormous toad that can grow to as much as 9 inches (23 centimeters) long from snout to rump and weigh up to 2.2 pounds (1.5 kilograms). (R. Andrew Odum/ Peter Arnold, Inc.)

Geographic range: The marine toad naturally occurs in Mexico, Central America, South America, and southern Texas in the United States, but people have introduced it to many other places around the world, including Hawaii, Japan, the Philippines, Australia, and numerous islands of the West Indies. It is now a pest species in many countries.

Habitat: In its native areas within South, Central, and North America, the marine toad prefers to make its home in fields and open forests that have at one time lost their trees, perhaps to logging or to fires. It naturally breeds in ponds, at the edges of lakes, and in small pools that form in rainy parts of the year and dry up later on. This toad, however, is very adaptable. This means that it can adjust to live in other places, too. This has helped the toad move into new areas, including villages and towns, and make its home there.

Diet: The marine toad has a good appetite. It eats a wide variety of arthropods. It will sit down at night near a light in a town and spend hours flipping out its tongue to snap up insects that fly toward the light. It will also devour ants, cockroaches, and many other types of insects wherever it can find them. Besides arthropods, marine toads have a reputation for gobbling down cat food and dog food from the feeding dishes of family pets. They are also known to sometimes eat snakes, frogs, and even small mammals, like mice.

Behavior and reproduction: Marine toads often spend their days grouped together in an out-of-the-way spot. They become active at night, which is when they do the bulk of their hunting. Sometimes, they travel quite a distance at night. Scientists are not sure how they do it, but the toads are always able to find their way back home. In the spring mating season, male marine toads move to water, sometimes even swimming pools, and begin calling for females. They usually prefer a shallow spot on the shore of a pond or small lake, or at the edge of a marsh. Here, a male pushes up on his front legs and makes his call, which is a long, low trill that may last ten or twenty seconds. When many of them call at once, the sound is something like a tractor engine. When a female approaches a male, he climbs onto her back, and grasps her behind her front legs. The two toads may swim about with the male still riding on the female's back until she finishes laying her eggs. One female may lay a string of twenty-five thousand eggs, sometimes more, and a single string may stretch nearly 10 feet long. In about two weeks, the eggs hatch into small, black tadpoles. The tadpoles may group together in schools, just as fish do, until they turn into toadlets.

Marine toads and people: In 1935, people brought the toad to Australia with the hopes that it would eat a type of beetle that was destroying the sugar cane crop. The toads, which got the nickname cane toad, found plenty to eat besides the beetles. The toads bred quickly, and since they had very few predators, soon became pests themselves. The toads are still very common in Australia. One of the reasons that people in that country dislike the toads is that pet dogs sometimes try to eat them. The poison in the toad's skin can cause illness and sometimes death.

Conservation status: The World Conservation Union (IUCN) does not list this species as being at risk, but rather notes that it is becoming more numerous and spreading to more places around the world. The toad's skin poison can make other organisms sick and even kill the eggs and tadpoles of other frogs that share water with marine toads and their tadpoles. ■

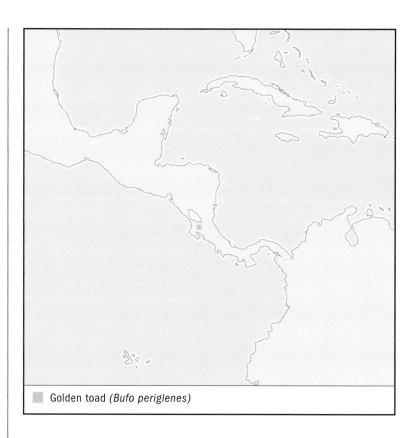

Golden toad (*Bufo periglenes*)

GOLDEN TOAD
Bufo periglenes

Physical characteristics: Only male golden toads are golden, and they actually are more orange than gold. Some people even call them orange toads instead. The females are very dark green, almost black, with red markings. Both males and females have thin, bony-looking bodies, much different than many of the plump toads in this family. Their front and hind legs are quite thin. Besides their colors, males and females are different in size. The females are the larger of the two, growing to 1.7 to 2.2 inches (4.2 to 5.6 centimeters) long from snout to rump. The males usually reach 1.5 to 1.9 inches (3.9 to 4.8 centimeters) in length.

Geographic range: Now extinct, golden toads once lived along a mountain ridge in the Monteverde Cloud Forest Preserve of

Only male golden toads are golden, and they actually are more orange than gold. Some people even call them orange toads instead. The females are very dark green, almost black, with red markings. (Illustration by Brian Cressman. Reproduced by permission.)

northwestern Costa Rica. For this reason, some people call it the Monteverde toad.

Habitat: Golden toads lived in mountain rainforests 4,920 to 5,250 feet (1,500 to 1,600 meters) above sea level.

Diet: Scientists had not yet learned about its diet before it became extinct in 1989.

Behavior and reproduction: The studies of this toad were mainly done during the breeding season, so very little is known about its behavior outside of mating and egg-laying. When heavy rains fell in the rainforest where this toad lived, hundreds of males would appear in groups. Scientists are not sure whether the males called. They did, however, notice that the number of males always outnumbered the females at a breeding site. Often, when a male would climb onto the back of a female to mate, one or more other males would begin wrestling with the first for the chance to push him off. If they were successful, one of these males would hop on the female, which would start yet another battle. The females laid their eggs in strings, and the eggs hatched into 1.2-inch (3-centimeter) tadpoles.

Golden toads and people: Following the extinction of this species, scientists became very concerned about the disappearance of frogs and toads around the world. The golden toad now serves as a symbol for amphibian conservation efforts.

Conservation status: Although scientists had seen large mating populations of the golden toad until 1987, its numbers dropped greatly in 1988 when only two females and eight males appeared at their normal breeding site. In 1989, a single, lone male arrived for mating season. He was the last golden toad ever seen. Although scientists do not know for sure, they think that infection with the chytrid fungus, pollution, and/or global warming, combined with the very small area in which they lived, may have caused the species to die out. ■

FOR MORE INFORMATION

Books:

Badger, David. *Frogs.* Stillwater, MN: Voyageur Press, 2000.

Crump, Martha L. *In Search of the Golden Frog.* Chicago: University of Chicago Press, 2000.

Halliday, Tim, and Kraig Adler, eds. *The Encyclopedia of Reptiles and Amphibians (Smithsonian Handbooks).* New York: Facts on File, 1991.

Inger, Robert F., and Robert B. Stuebing. *A Field Guide to the Frogs of Borneo.* Kota Kinabalu: Natural History Publications, 1997.

Mattison, Chris. *Frogs and Toads of the World.* New York: Facts on File Publications, 1987.

Meyer, John R., and Carol F. Foster. *A Guide to the Frogs and Toads of Belize.* Malabar, FL: Krieger Publishing Co., 1996.

Miller, Sara Swan. *Frogs and Toads: The Leggy Leapers.* New York: Franklin Watts, 2000.

Savage, Jay M. *The Amphibians and Reptiles of Costa Rica.* Chicago: University of Chicago Press, 2002.

Showler, Dave. *Frogs and Toads: A Golden Guide.* New York: St. Martin's Press, 2004.

Tyning, Thomas. *A Guide to Amphibians and Reptiles.* Boston: Little, Brown and Company, 1990.

Periodicals:

"Look Out for Toads on Roads!" *Current Events, a Weekly Reader publication.* April 25, 1994 (vol. 93): page 3.

O'Neill, William J. "Guard Your Garden With a Hungry Toad." *Child Life.* April-May 2002 (vol. 81): page 10.

Web sites:

"American Toad." *eNature, National Wildlife Federation.* http://www.enature.com/fieldguide/showSpeciesRECNUM.asp?recnum=AR0006 (accessed on April 12, 2005).

"*Ansonia longidigita.*" *CalPhotos.* http://elib.cs.berkeley.edu/cgi/img_query?query_src=&enlarge=0000+0000+0903+0287 (accessed on April 9, 2005).

"Cane Toad, Giant American Toad, Marine Toad." *BBC.* http://www.bbc.co.uk/nature/wildfacts/factfiles/392.shtml (accessed on April 12, 2005).

"Colorado River Toad." *Yahooligans! Animals.* http://yahooligans.yahoo.com/content/animals/species/4529.html (accessed on April 12, 2005).

"Giant Marine Toad." *Utah's Hogle Zoo.* http://www.xmission.com/hoglezoo/animals/view.php?id=21 (accessed on April 12, 2005).

"Toothless Predator." *American Museum of Natural History.* http://www.amnh.org/exhibitions/frogs/featured/toothless.php (accessed on April 9, 2005).

POISON FROGS

Dendrobatidae

Class: Amphibia

Order: Anura

Family: Dendrobatidae

Number of species: 207 species

CHAPTER

PHYSICAL CHARACTERISTICS

Poison frogs are known for the very poisonous skin that many of them have. Actually, all frogs have poison glands, or small groups of cells, that ooze poison. In most species, the poison is very mild and, at most, only serves to make the frog taste bad. In some of the species in this family, however, the poison is far more potent and may even be deadly. The skin of the golden dart-poison frog, for instance, contains an especially dangerous poison, or toxin. Even the tiniest of droplets of this toxin in a predator's bloodstream can be fatal. Not all of the poison frog species are equally toxic, and some have no more poison than most other frogs in the world. Even within one species, different individuals may have different levels of toxin.

Scientists think that the especially toxic poison frogs may not actually make their toxins themselves, but instead get them by eating poisonous insects that, in turn, get their toxins by eating poisonous plants. The insects can eat the poisonous plants, and the frogs can eat the poisonous insects without having any health problems. When these especially toxic poison frogs are taken out of their natural habitat, placed in an aquarium, and fed non-poisonous food, the frogs eventually lose their high levels of toxins. The word toxicity (tox-ISS-ih-tee) means the level of toxins.

The toxic poison frogs are very colorful. These bright shades, called warning colors, caution predators against eating the frogs. The typical strawberry poison frog, for example, stands out with a bold red body and vivid blue legs. The Brazil nut poison frog has a black body with white to cream-colored spots and blotches on its back and red patches on its front and hind legs. People often describe these lovely little frogs as "jewels."

Those poison frogs that do not have especially toxic skin typically have much more drab colors, such as browns, tans, and olive greens. Often, these colors are in patterns that blend in with the frogs' surroundings. Rather than alerting predators to their presence, their colors camouflage them from predators. Stephen's rocket frog and the Trinidad poison frog are examples. Both are brown with darker brown stripes on the sides of the body and have dark banded legs.

In some species, like the strawberry poison frog, individuals may come in different colors. Those that live in one part of Panama are red and blue as described above, but those that live in other parts of the country may be green, yellow, or orange and may have a variety of patterns on their backs, including stripes or spots. Trinidad poison frogs are an example of a species with different-looking males and females. Both the males and the females have brown backs, but the males have gray throats with a black collar, while the females have the black collar but have bright yellow throats.

Perhaps the most unusual species in its appearance is the imitating poison frog. This small frog takes on a whole new look depending on its neighbors. If it lives near a Zimmermann's poison frog, the imitating frog looks like that species with its black-spotted yellow back, black-spotted blue legs, and blue belly. If it lives in the same area as the Amazon or Amazonian poison frog, which is an orange or yellow frog with long black stripes or spots, the imitating poison frog has that pattern. In addition, when the imitating frog shares a habitat with the red-headed poison frog, which is also known as the crowned poison frog, it has the half-orange or -red, half-black body of that species. The imitating frog is the only frog or amphibian known to copy, or mimic, the appearance of another amphibian. The imitating

A CUP OF WATER

The tadpoles of some species of poison frogs can survive in even the tiniest pools of water. Tadpoles of the very small Stephen's rocket frog and the Brazil nut frog are some of the most amazing. The female Stephen's rocket frog lays her three to six eggs in the water within cup-shaped leaves that lie on the forest floor. The male stands guard, but does not carry the tadpoles to a bigger pool of water. The eggs hatch into tadpoles in the small puddle inside the leaf, and the tadpoles remain there until they turn into froglets. In the Brazil nut frog, the males carry the eggs to water, but that water is the tiny puddle that forms inside the empty shell of a Brazil nut.

frog and all three of the species it mimics are highly toxic, but they are not close relatives of one another.

Regardless of the types of toxins in their skin or their colors, all poison frogs have a few things in common. They have powerful, although short, hind legs for leaping and, in some species, for climbing. They have thick pads of skin on the tops of their front and rear toes. The vast majority of them are also quite small. Most grow to 0.75 to 1.5 inches (1.9 to 3.8 centimeters) long from the tip of the snout to the end of the rump. The Brazilian poison frog and the blue-bellied poison frog are especially tiny. Female Brazilian poison frogs reach 0.68 to 0.8 inches (1.72 to 2.03 centimeters) long, and males are even smaller at 0.63 to 0.71 inches (1.6 to 1.8 centimeters) in length. Female blue-bellied poison frogs grow to 0.47 to 0.61 inches (1.19 to 1.55 centimeters), while the males reach just 0.47 to 0.59 inches (1.19 to 1.49 centimeters) in length. The Venezuelan skunk frog is one of the largest poison frogs. Females of this olive-green frog can grow to 2.5 inches (6.35 centimeters) long.

GEOGRAPHIC RANGE

Poison frogs live in central to southern parts of Central America, including Nicaragua, Costa Rica, and Panama. They also live throughout much of northern to central South America, as far south as Bolivia and southern Brazil. The green and black poison frog, also known as the green poison frog, is the only poison frog to have jumped from its native home in Central and South America to Hawaii. In 1932, people brought the frogs from Panama to the Hawaiian island of Oahu with the idea that the frogs would eat some introduced insects on the island. The frogs liked their new home and still live on Oahu today.

HABITAT

Most of the frogs in this family live in moist forests or rainforests that have never been cleared. Such uncut forests are called primary forests. A few can also survive in old, now-overgrown pastures. Among the poison frogs, only one species spends its life in the water. This is the Venezuelan skunk frog that lives in small streams and has fully webbed rear toes to help it swim.

DIET

Poison frogs typically eat small insects and other arthropods (AR-throe-pawds), which are animals that have jointed legs and no backbones. Some of the common arthropods in the typical poison frog's diet include mites, ants, and small spiders, flies, and/or beetles. Researchers have been particularly interested in why the especially toxic poison frogs are so poisonous. In 2004, a group of scientists announced that ants may be part of the reason for at least some of the frogs' toxicity. The ants have the same toxins as the frogs. When the frogs eat the ants, the frogs take on that poison and become toxic themselves. Although the scientists are not sure what makes the ants poisonous, they suspect that the ants eat poisonous plants that make the poisons.

BEHAVIOR AND REPRODUCTION

Almost all of the poison frogs are active during the daytime, usually at dawn and late in the afternoon, and especially when it rains. The most toxic species hop about in plain view of potential predators, but the predators normally leave them alone to avoid a dangerous mouthful of poison. The frogs that do not have dangerous toxins in their skin are typically dull-colored and blend in with their surroundings. This camouflage usually keeps them out of their predators' sights. If a predator does spot a frog, the poison frogs have strong legs to help them leap away. Some of the frogs also are very good climbers and can avoid ground-living predators by scrambling up bushes and trees. The family name, Dendrobatidae, actually comes from two words that mean tree and walker in Greek. The Brazilian poison frogs and the polka dot poison frogs are two species that spend their lives in the trees.

The Venezuelan skunk frog is unusual, in part, because it is active at night. This species has an odd but effective defense against predators. As its common name suggests, it has a very strong, skunklike odor that wards off attackers. Scientists are interested in this species, which was discovered in the 1980s, because it may help them figure out which other families of frogs are most closely related to the poison frogs. Although scientists are not sure, they think the poison frogs' nearest relatives may be the true toads in the family Bufonidae, or the leptodactylid frogs.

The males of many species set up and defend territories against other males. These territories can be important during the mating season. Studies of strawberry poison frogs, for example, have shown that the males with the best territories are the best at attracting females. In this case, the best territories are those that are larger and have more tall places where the males can call to females. Often, male poison frogs defend their territories with a certain type of call, called an encounter call, that tells other males to stay away. In some species, like Stephen's rocket frog, the encounter call is different from the call that they use to attract females. In other poison frogs, the two calls sound much alike and may even be the same. The Trinidad poison frog is different because the females instead of the males are the ones who set up and defend territories. The females cannot call, so they defend their territories by rippling their bright yellow throats while sitting up tall in a high spot of the territory. In the green poison frog, the female does not set up territories, but she will fight with other females that approach her mate.

The breeding time for poison frogs is commonly during the rainy season, which runs from about November to April, although it may be a bit longer or shorter in some areas. Males call the most early in the day; then they quiet down. If the day is rainy, however, they may start calling again later in the afternoon. Some species, like Stephen's rocket frog, may call any time of day if it is raining. The males call from land. Some call from the leaf-covered ground, others from a hole in a tree trunk, and some species from plants that grow on the sides of trees.

For many species, scientists have never seen the males and females mate. In others, like the harlequin poison frogs, they have a good deal of detail. In this species, the male calls to attract a female. When she comes toward him, he continues calling while hopping away and leading her to the mating site, which is under leaves on the forest floor. This species is one of many, including the green poison frog, the blue-bellied poison frog, and the strawberry poison frog, that lay their eggs in leaves lying on the ground. The female blue-toed rocket frog places her eggs inside rolled or folded leaves. Other species of poison frogs lay their eggs in the trees. The female Brazilian poison frog, for instance, lays her eggs in small, wet tree holes just above a water puddle inside the hole. All of the poison frogs lay their eggs out of the water, except possibly the Venezuelan skunk frog. No one has seen where this water-loving frog lays its eggs. The female may lay them in the water, or she may come out to lay the eggs on land.

Some of the poison frogs have only a few eggs at a time. The female blue-bellied poison frog usually lays just two eggs, the female Brazilian poison frog lays two or three, and the strawberry poison frog lays two to six in a clutch. Many additional species also have small clutches. Other frogs in this family, including the blue-toed rocket and phantasmal poison frog, have larger clutches. The female blue-toed rocket usually lays about nineteen eggs, while the female phantasmal poison frog lays between fifteen and forty eggs in a single clutch.

In most other types of frogs, both adults leave after the eggs are laid. In poison frogs, however, either the male or the female stays behind with the young until they hatch into tadpoles. Occasionally, both adults stay with the eggs. In the green poison frog, for example, the male continues to check on the eggs during the two weeks it takes them to hatch. During this time, he turns the eggs, adds water to them to keep them moist, and removes any fungus that may have started to grow on them. The male is also the caregiver in the blue-bellied poison frogs, the Amazonian poison frogs, the phantasmal poison frogs, the Trinidad poison frogs, and others. The harlequin poison frog is one of several species in which the female stays with the eggs. In a few species, including the strawberry poison frog and the Brazilian poison frog, the adults share the job.

Part of the care includes carrying the tadpoles to water where they will continue to grow and develop into froglets. In most cases, the adult sits in the middle of the hatching eggs, and the tadpoles squirm onto the adult's back. The adult then moves over to water, sometimes spending quite some time searching for the perfect spot, and drops off the tadpoles. In some species, the adult carries only one tadpole at a time and has to make a few trips from the nest to the water before he or she has moved the entire family. Once the adult has delivered all of the tadpoles to the water, the tadpoles are on their own. Among green poison frogs, one male may mate with and have young by more than one female during one breeding season. Since he is the caregiver for the eggs, he has to watch over several nests at once. Sometimes, he is not successful, and some of the tadpoles die before he can get all of the young to water.

In the strawberry poison frog, the male cares for the eggs by keeping them moist and clean, but the female takes over when the eggs are ready to hatch. She carries one tadpole at a time to plants that have puddles of water laying at the base of their leaves or filling a cup that forms from their overlapping leaves. These small puddles do not contain much, if anything, for the tadpoles to eat, so the female comes back to her growing young every five days or so to feed them. The food she leaves is additional eggs that she lays. The eggs are infertile (in-FER-tul), which means that they will never develop into young. The tadpoles eat the infertile eggs until they grow and mature into froglets.

POISON FROGS AND PEOPLE

Many of the colorful poison frogs are common in the pet trade. They have also become popular attractions in exhibits at aquariums and zoos. Some local people in their native lands have dipped darts into the skin toxins of some of the especially poisonous species. Using blowguns, they shoot the darts at small animals they were hunting. The darts would kill the animals. Scientists, on the other hand, have become interested in these frogs' powerful toxins for the possible development of new pain-relieving drugs.

CONSERVATION STATUS

The World Conservation Union (IUCN) lists seventy-nine species—thirty-eight percent of all of the species in the family—as being at some risk. It also considers ninety-three others—another forty-five percent—as Data Deficient, which means that too little information is available to make a judgment about the threat of extinction.

Of the seventy-nine at-risk species, the IUCN lists nineteen as Critically Endangered and facing an extremely high risk of extinction in the wild. Several of these species, including the skunk frog and the Bloody Bay poison frog, have had huge drops in number during recent years. In just three generations, which would include the grandparents, parents, and children, the number of Bloody Bay poison frogs has plunged by eighty percent. In other words, for every one hundred individuals in the grandparents' generation, this species has only twenty individuals left in the children's generation. The number of skunk frogs also dropped by eighty percent in just a ten-year period. In the skunk frog's case, the decline is probably due to a loss of their habitat as people have built roads, farms, and ranches. In addition, a dry spell has lowered the level of water where the frogs mate and may have hurt the young. In the case of the Bloody Bay frog, scientists are not certain, but they think infection with a type of fungus may have been to blame for the frogs' disappearance. This fungus, called chytrid (KIT-rid) fungus, has killed members of many different frog species worldwide and may be hurting some of the other poison frogs, too.

Many of the Critically Endangered poison frogs are very rare and live in small areas that are being destroyed or are under other threats from human activities, like the clearing of land through logging or the use of farm pesticides that are dangerous to frogs, including their eggs and tadpoles.

Besides the nineteen Critically Endangered species, thirty are Endangered and facing a very high risk of extinction in the wild; sixteen are Vulnerable and facing a high risk of extinction in the wild; and fourteen are Near Threatened and at risk of becoming threatened with extinction in the future. Some, like the splendid poison frog, were once common but are now extremely rare and may even be extinct. The IUCN currently lists the splendid poison frog as Endangered, noting its popularity in the pet trade and the loss of its habitat as likely causes for its much lower numbers. Scientists are unsure whether any of the frogs still live in the wild.

Golden dart-poison frog (*Phyllobates terribilis*)

GOLDEN DART-POISON FROG
Phyllobates terribilis

Physical characteristics: Golden dart-poison frogs, also known as golden poison frogs, come in different colors. In one, called the golden phase, the frogs have a yellow to orange yellow back and head and large dark eyes. Their legs may be yellow, orange yellow, or slightly greenish. In the mint green phase, the frogs' backs and legs are a very light greenish white color. The undersides of golden or mint phase golden frogs may have a few dark marks here and there, especially on the legs where they meet the body. Their backs are often quite smooth and shiny, but their back legs may have small bumps on them. Sometimes, their backs are also covered with tiny bumps. They have strong back legs for leaping and thin front legs. The head is short and becomes narrower toward the tip of the snout, giving it a triangular shape. They have a wide mouth that crosses the snout and reaches

around the sides of the head, past each eye to a spot below the eardrum, which can be seen as a round area behind and below each eye. Females are usually a bit larger than males, but only barely. Females usually are 1.6 to 1.85 inches (4 to 4.7 centimeters) long from snout to rump, while males are usually 1.5 to 1.8 inches (3.8 to 4.5 centimeters) in length.

Geographic range: The golden dart-poison frog lives in Cauca, Colombia, which is in northwestern South America.

Habitat: It is found on land in lowland rainforests along the west coast of Colombia up to 656 feet (200 meters) above sea level. The tadpoles hatch in freshwater, but the exact kind of water body is unknown.

Diet: Adults eat various small arthropods, including insects.

Behavior and reproduction: Rather than climbing into trees like some of the other poison frogs do, the golden dart-poison frog stays on the ground. It is active during the daytime, when it hops about in plain view. It is one of the most poisonous animals on Earth. The poison in its skin is so powerful that even a tiny amount in another animal's bloodstream, including that of a human being, is enough to cause death. Called batrachotoxin (buh-TRAK-oh-tox-in), the poison attacks the nervous system.

Golden dart-poison frogs and people: This frog can be seen in the pet trade, but it is not common. Some local people use the poison in the frog's skin to make deadly darts. The golden dart-poison frog is one of only three species of frogs—the other two are closely related species—that are used to make the darts.

Conservation status: The World Conservation Union (IUCN) considers the golden dart-poison frog to be Endangered, which means that it faces a very high risk of extinction in the wild. Although the frog is common where it lives, it lives only in a tiny area and only in places where the forest has never been cut. Conservationists are not sure whether it could survive if the trees were ever removed and are concerned because forests near the frog are already falling as people remove trees for lumber and to make way for farms or buildings. Conservationists also think that the spray poisons farmers use to kill crop-eating insects could hurt the frogs. So far, the frog's habitat is not protected from logging, but it is now illegal to capture the frogs from the wild. ■

Phantasmal poison frog *(Epipedobates tricolor)*

PHANTASMAL POISON FROG
Epipedobates tricolor

Physical characteristics: Phantasmal poison frogs are dark brown or brick red with three cream-colored, yellow, or light green stripes running from the head to the rump. The center stripe widens out at the front of the head to cover the whole snout, and the two side stripes may also come far enough forward to blend into this snout blotch. Sometimes, the stripes are broken into dotted lines or blotches. The green, yellow, or cream color also appears on the front and back legs in spots. The frog has long hind legs for leaping and fairly long but thin front legs. It has two large eyes on its head, which slopes toward the front. Often the frogs have a short green, yellow, or cream-colored line under each eye. The underside, including the belly and throat, has numerous green or cream blotches that sometimes almost completely color the underside. Females and males are nearly the

same size. As adults, females usually reach about 0.8 to 1.1 inch (2.1 to 2.7 centimeters) long from snout to rump. Males typically reach slightly less than an inch (2.5 centimeters).

Geographic range: Phantasmal poison frogs live in southwestern Ecuador and northwestern Peru to the west of the Andes Mountains.

Habitat: Adults live on land in mountain valleys. Although they survive in wet or dry areas, they usually remain near streams. Tadpoles develop in streams or small pools of water.

Diet: Adult phantasmal poison frogs eat various small arthropods, including insects.

Behavior and reproduction: Scientists know little about this species outside of its breeding behavior. Mating occurs on land, as it does in the other poison frog species, but phantasmal poison frogs mate differently. While the male mates by climbing onto the back of a female, he does not hold onto her near her front or back legs, as nearly all other frogs do. Instead, he grips her with his front legs around her head. From this awkward-looking position, the female lays fifteen to forty eggs. Afterward, the female leaves, but the male stays behind with the eggs and watches over them. As each egg hatches into a tadpole, the tadpole scrambles up the male's leg and onto his back, and he carries the tadpole to a nearby stream or pool. The tadpole swims off, and the male returns to the hatching eggs to pick up the next tadpole. He continues until he has carried all the young to the water. The tadpoles develop into froglets in the water.

Phantasmal poison frogs and people: The poison in this frog's skin, while very dangerous, has helped scientists to design effective painkillers for human patients. By studying the frog's poison, which is two hundred times more powerful than the drug morphine (MORE-feen), scientists have made drugs that work in the same way that the poison does, but are not unsafe.

Conservation status: The World Conservation Union considers the phantasmal poison frog to be Endangered, which means that it faces a very high risk of extinction in the wild. This species lives in only seven spots on mountains in part of Ecuador, but it once lived over a larger area. In the remaining populations, the number of adult frogs is continuing to drop. Its small habitat is at risk because the land is being developed for farming, and because farming chemicals are polluting the water in the frogs' habitat. Conservationists are not sure, but they think that the frogs might also be at risk from people who collect them for the pet trade or from infection with chytrid fungus. This fungus has killed many different kinds of frogs around the world. ■

Blue-toed rocket frog (*Colostethus caeruleodactylus*)

BLUE-TOED ROCKET FROG
Colostethus caeruleodactylus

Physical characteristics: The blue-toed rocket frogs are named for their blue toes. During the breeding season, the males have blue front toes and blue pads on their back toes. Females have blue pads on both front and back toes during the breeding season, but their front toes are not all blue, as they are in males. Besides the blue toes and/or toe pads, the frogs have brown backs and heads and white chins and bellies. They have long hind legs and short front legs. The head narrows to a rather triangular-shaped snout. Females may be just a bit bigger than the males. Adult females usually grow to 0.59 to 0.67 inches (1.5 to 1.7 centimeters) from snout to rump, while males typically reach no more than 0.63 inches (1.6 centimeters).

The blue-toed rocket frogs are named for their blue toes. During the breeding season, the males have blue front toes and blue pads on their back toes. Females have blue pads on both front and back toes during the breeding season, but their front toes are not all blue, as they are in males. (Illustration by Joseph E. Trumpey. Reproduced by permission.)

Geographic range: Blue-toed rocket frogs have only been found in one place: about 25 miles (40 kilometers) south of Manaus, Amazonas, Brazil.

Habitat: The frogs live in a small piece of tropical rainforest valley that is flooded with water during the rainy season. The floods rush water into rivers of the valley, causing the rivers to overflow into small streams and create deep pools in the streams. The frogs live among the dead leaves that cover the slopes of forest floor above the streams. Their tadpoles develop in the deep stream pools.

Diet: Adult blue-toed rocket frogs eat various small arthropods, including insects.

Behavior and reproduction: Blue-toed rocket frogs live on land. The males set up territories that are about one thousand square feet (ten square meters). To keep others away, a male will give a short, loud call. Males and females mate on land during the rainy season, which lasts from January through April. Each female lays her eggs on the forest floor, hiding them away in folded or rolled leaves. The male then stays with his eggs, usually about nineteen in each clutch, even after they hatch into tadpoles. When the rainy season ends and the ground begins to dry up, the male carries all of the tadpoles to deep pools in the streams, where the tadpoles continue to grow.

Blue-toed rocket frogs and people: Very few people have ever seen this frog.

Conservation status: Too little information is available about this frog to make a judgment about the threat of extinction, so the World Conservation Union (IUCN) lists it as Data Deficient. Scientists only recently discovered this frog, naming it in 2001. They found it in just one spot, where it was very common, and have not yet found it anywhere else. The scientists believe that the logging of the forest would cause it to become extinct. The frogs' forest is on private property and therefore not protected from logging. ■

FOR MORE INFORMATION

Books:

Badger, David. *Frogs.* Stillwater, MN: Voyageur Press, 2000.

Fridell, Ron. *The Search for Poison-Dart Frogs.* New York: Franklin Watts, 2001.

Halliday, Tim, and Kraig Adler, eds. *The Encyclopedia of Reptiles and Amphibians (Smithsonian Handbooks).* New York: Facts on File, 1991.

Heselhaus, Ralf. *Poison-Arrow Frogs: Their Natural History and Care in Captivity.* London: Blandford, 1992.

Mattison, Chris. *Frogs and Toads of the World.* New York: Facts on File Publications, 1987.

Miller, Sara Swan. *Frogs and Toads: The Leggy Leapers.* New York: Franklin Watts, 2000.

Patent, Dorothy Hinshaw. *Frogs, Toads, Salamanders, and How They Reproduce.* New York: Holiday House, 1975.

Showler, Dave. *Frogs and Toads: A Golden Guide.* New York: St. Martin's Press, 2004.

Walls, Jerry G. *Poison Frogs of the Family Dendrobatidae: Jewels of the Rainforest.* Neptune City, NJ: TFH Publications, 1994.

Periodicals:

Jenkins, Jeanette. "The Poison Dart Frog." *Science News,* February-March 2002 (vol. 7): page 10.

Milius, Susan. "Toxin Takeout: Frogs Borrow Poison for Skin From Ants." *Science News,* May 8, 2004 (vol. 165): page 291.

"Strawberry Poison Dart Frog Born at Bristol Zoo Gardens." *Current Science, a Weekly Reader publication,* October 10, 2003 (volume 89): page 14.

Web sites:

"Blue Poison Frog." *Henson Robinson Zoo.* http://www.hensonrobinsonzoo.org/a002.html (accessed on April 14, 2005).

"*Dendrobates. WhoZoo.* http://www.whozoo.org/Intro98/jenntrev/jendex3.html (accessed on April 14, 2005).

"Frog Chemist Creates a Deadlier Poison." *Science News for Kids.* http://www.sciencenewsforkids.org-articles-20030910-Note3.asp (accessed on April 14, 2005).

"Frogs Get Poison from Ants." *Science News for Kids.* http://www.sciencenewsforkids.org-articles-20040512-Note3.asp (accessed on April 14, 2005).

"*Phyllobates terribilis* 'Mint'." *Frog of the Month, Arachnokulture.* http://www.pumilio.com/frogofthemonth/december2001.htm (accessed on April 14, 2005).

"Poison Dart Frog (*Dendrobates pumilio*)." *Basic Science and Remote Sensing Initiative, Michigan State University.* http://www.bsrsi.msu.edu/rfrc/tour/dendrobates.html (accessed on April 14, 2005).

"Poison Dart Frog (*Dendrobates pumilio*)." *Woodland Park Zoo.* http://www.zoo.org/educate/fact_sheets/psn_frog/psn_frog.htm (accessed on April 14, 2005).

"Poison Dart Frogs." *Smithsonian National Zoological Park.* http://nationalzoo.si.edu/Animals/Amazonia/Facts/fact-poisondartfrog.cfm (accessed on April 14, 2005).

"Poison Dart Frogs, Mantellas, etc." *All About Frogs.* http://allaboutfrogs.org/info/species/poison.html (accessed on April 14, 2005).

family

PHYSICAL CHARACTERISTICS

Ruthven's frog is a metallic brown color, sometimes yellow- or gray-brown, with darker marks and lighter yellow-brown or gold stripes down each side of the back. The back of its long body is scattered with tiny spikes, or spicules (SPIK-yuhlz), that are partly buried in the skin. The spicules in males are larger than those in females. Because of the spicules, which look somewhat like warts, people often describe this frog as toad-like. It has large eyes that bulge from each side of its head. The head becomes flatter toward the front. Its front and back legs are thin, and the toes end in rounded pads. The front legs often have noticeable light-colored spots that extend onto the chest and throat. Light-colored spots also cover the lower part of its head around the mouth. Often, the sides of the body and parts of the legs have a pink, see-through appearance.

Males have a dark, unspotted area on the throat that remains hidden except when they call. During calling, this area, called a vocal sac, blows up to a large size—at least the size of the head and sometimes much larger. The females grow slightly larger than the males. Females typically reach 0.85 to 1.20 inches (2.2 to 3.1 centimeters) long from snout to rump, and males usually grow to 0.8 to 1 inch (2.1 to 2.5 centimeters) in length.

Discovered in 1926, the single species of Ruthven's frog has at one time or another been listed in five different frog families, including the true toads, the glass frogs, the leptodactylid frogs, the tree frogs, and its own separate family, as it is listed here. Scientists have found no fossils to study. The confusion in the listing of this frog's family comes from the fact that the frog has some features of all of the different families. For example, its toe bones are T-shaped at the tips, which scientists once thought was like the toes of the glass frogs or possibly the tree frogs. Studies since then showed that the toe bones of Ruthven's frogs are actually slightly different than those of either the glass or the tree frogs.

During the mating season, male Ruthven's frogs call from plants and trees above ponds, and females lay their eggs in the water, which is the same situation as seen in the tree frogs. Like true toads, Ruthven's frogs have no teeth. In fact, the scientific name of Ruthven's frogs, *Allophryne*, means "other toad," because it was thought to be a new kind of true toad.

Ruthven's frog's full scientific name is *Allophryne ruthveni*. Like many other species of plants and animals, the second part of its name refers to a person or to the place where it was collected. In this case, the name refers to Alexander Ruthven, a noted herpetologist (her-peh-TOL-eh-jist) who was very active in the first half of the twentieth century. A herpetologist is a person who studies amphibians and reptiles. Ruthven, who was curator of the Division of Reptiles and Amphibians at the University of Michigan Museum of Zoology, led eighteen of the museum's expeditions to places throughout the United States, Mexico, Central America, and South America.

HERPETOLOGIST EXPLORERS

Helen Thompson Gaige, who in 1926 was the first person scientifically to describe Ruthven's frog, was one of the earliest, well-known, female herpetologists. Gaige, who lived from 1886 to 1976, named many new species of frogs, especially those from Central and South America. Ruthven's frog is a South American species. Her career included positions as scientific assistant and then curator of the Division of Reptiles and Amphibians at the University of Michigan Museum of Zoology (UMMZ). Ruthven's frog carries the name of Alexander Ruthven, another respected herpetologist from the early twentieth century. He traveled through much of the New World studying amphibians and reptiles. Ruthven was curator of the UMMZ Division of Reptiles and Amphibians from 1906 to 1936, the museum director from 1913 to 1929, and president of the University of Michigan from 1929 to 1951.

In 2002, a group of scientists compared the DNA of Ruthven's frogs to the DNA of other frogs. DNA is a string of chemicals that provides the instructions for making a living thing. By comparing the DNA of different organisms, scientists can tell how similar they are. The comparison showed that Ruthven's frogs may be most closely related to the glass frogs and perhaps should be considered members of that family. Until more studies are done, however, many scientists list Ruthven's frogs as the lone members of its own family, called Allophrynidae, while some others still place it in the family Hylidae. In 2003, scientists

discovered what they believe may be a second species of Ruthven's frog. It is black with bright white and yellow spots and has two bulging eyes, one on each side of its head.

GEOGRAPHIC RANGE

Ruthven's frog was first found in Tukeit Hill below Kaiteur Falls in Guyana in northern South America. It has since been seen in many parts of South America, including north-central Brazil, French Guiana, Guyana, Suriname, and Venezuela. Since scientists have not yet fully explored the area around the Amazon River where this frog lives, other populations of Ruthven's frogs probably remain undiscovered. In addition, a possible second species of Ruthven's frog has been discovered in Peru.

HABITAT

Ruthven's frogs live in lowland forests rather than forests on hillsides or in the mountains. This frog usually goes no higher on hillsides than about 656 feet (200 meters) above sea level and stays in forests that have not been logged but, nevertheless, are not too thick with plants and trees. Throughout the year, they typically stay in areas near rivers and streams. During the rainy season, they group together around low spots in the forest that fill with rain or overflowing river water.

DIET

Scientists have not studied this small frog in enough detail to learn what it eats. If it follows the pattern of the glass frogs and many other types of frogs, however, it eats small insects.

Ruthven's frog *(Allophryne ruthveni)*

BEHAVIOR AND REPRODUCTION

They are nocturnal (nahk-TER-nuhl), which means that they are active at night. During this time, they move around the forests near rivers and streams. They climb through trees and large bushes and onto the leaves of branches that may be several feet (1 to 3 meters) above the forest floor. Sometimes they sit in bromeliads (BRO-mee-lee-adds), which are plants that grow in warm, usually tropical forests often on other plants. Many bromeliads have leaves that overlap into cup shapes that can hold water and are very attractive spots for frogs and insects.

One of the frog's predators is a snake known by its scientific name of *Leimadophis reginae*. Scientists learned about the snake's appetite for the frogs when they captured one of the snakes on the edge of a river in Suriname, which is in northern South America. They cut open the snake's stomach and found a pregnant female Ruthven's frog inside.

The rainy season in the part of South America where the Ruthven's frog lives lasts from about January to July, although it is shorter in some places. The rains create small pools of water in dips in the forest floor and also cause rivers and streams to overflow onto banks and into other small pools of water. As long as the rains continue, the pools stay wet, but when the rainy season ends, they start to dry up. Since the pools only remain wet for part of the year, they are called temporary pools. The frogs make use of these temporary pools. The males hop to the edges of the water, or sometimes onto the leaves of low-hanging tree and bush branches, and begin calling. The call is a string of short low notes that together sound like a trill. Researchers studied the call by making a recording as a male trilled. They were able to count eighteen notes per second in its trill. Many males may call from the same place. This kind of group singing is known as a chorus (KOR-us).

Scientists found an especially large chorus in a pond near Pará, which is in northern Brazil. The pond actually formed when rains flooded the Amazon River and its tributaries, which are the smaller rivers and streams that flow into the Amazon. One of the tributaries, the Rio Xingu, overflowed to make the pond. Only a few frogs called from the pond for two months, but on one night in March, several hundred frogs suddenly showed up. Apparently, the frogs waited to mate until the tributary had flooded enough to fill the pond with a great deal of water. This type of mating, which happens during a short period of time and includes a large number of frogs, is called explosive breeding.

To mate, the male grasps the female from behind and near her front legs. While the male is in this piggyback position, called amplexus (am-PLEK-sus), the female lays her eggs, which number in the hundreds, in the water. Scientists learned how many eggs they lay by capturing a pair of mating frogs, dropping them in a plastic bag, and then counting as the female laid three hundred eggs. None of the eggs lived to hatch, however, and scientists still do not know what the Ruthven's frog tadpoles look like.

RUTHVEN'S FROGS AND PEOPLE

People rarely see this frog in the wild, although it is actually quite common in the parts of South America where it lives. Scientists find it interesting because they do not know exactly where it fits in the family tree of all frog species. Once they find tadpoles or possibly a fossil of a frog, however, they may learn details that will help them decide if the Ruthven's frog should stay in its own family or should be included in another family, such as the glass frogs.

CONSERVATION STATUS

The World Conservation Union (IUCN) does not consider Ruthven's frog to be at risk. It lives in an area that is seldom visited by humans, and the frog is quite common there. The frog has not been studied well, however, and scientists are unsure where all of the populations are located. Some populations that have not yet been discovered may live in parts of the South American forest that are currently being logged.

FOR MORE INFORMATION

Books:

Caldwell, Janalee P. "Diversity of Amazonian Anurans: The Role of Systematics and Phylogeny in Identifying Macroecological and Evolutionary Patterns." In *Neotropical Biodiversity and Conservation,* edited by A. C. Gibson. Los Angeles: Mildred E. Mathias Botanical Garden Miscellaneous Publications, 1996.

Showler, Dave. *Frogs and Toads: A Golden Guide.* New York: St. Martin's Press, 2004.

Zug, George. *Herpetology: An Introductory Biology of Amphibians and Reptiles.* San Diego, CA: Academic Press, 1993.

Web sites:

"*Allophryne ruthveni.*" *Swissherp.* http://www.nouragues.cnrs.fr/NourAnimaux.htm (accessed on April 7, 2005).

"Genus *Allophryne.*" *Animal Diversity Web,* University of Michigan Museum of Zoology. http://animaldiversity.ummz.umich.edu/site/accounts/classification/Allophryne.html#Allophryne (accessed on April 7, 2005).

"Pictures of Ruthven's *Allophryne* (Allophrynidae)." *Swissherp.* http://www.swissherp.org/Amphibians/Allophrynidae/Allophrynidae.html (accessed on April 7, 2005).

"Rapid Biological Inventories." *The Field Museum.* http://fm2.fieldmuseum.org/rbi/results_per11.asp (accessed on April 7, 2005).

GLASS FROGS
Centrolenidae

Class: Amphibia

Order: Anura

Family: Centrolenidae

Number of species: 134 species

family

CHAPTER

phylum

class

subclass

order

monotypic order

suborder

▲ **family**

PHYSICAL CHARACTERISTICS

In many of the species of glass frogs, the beating heart, other working organs, blood vessels, and the bones inside are clearly visible through their see-through, or transparent, undersides. Even from the top in many species, the frogs' bodies have the look of frosted glass and sometimes provide a glimpse of the animals' inner workings. In fact, the descriptions of some species include the size of their organs. The view from the top-side is not as good as it is from the bottom, because the frog has thick muscles on its back that hide the organs from sight.

Most of the glass frogs are shades of green, although some are brown. Many have tiny spots, which are called ocelli (oh-CELL-ee). These ocelli in frogs should not be confused with the ocelli in insects. In insects, ocelli look like the spots on a frog's back, but they are actually tiny eyes. Lynch's Cochran frog, for instance, may be brownish green or tan and has black ocelli that are tipped in orange or yellow. It also has white warts. The Nicaraguan glass frog is green, sometimes with numerous black spots on its head, back, and legs. In the Atrato glass frog, the back is yellow green with small brown spots in all but a few large, round patches on its head, back, and legs. Regardless of their color or pattern, most glass frogs are extremely hard to see when they sit on green leaves. They almost look as if they melt into the leaves and become a part of them.

Since the bones are visible from the outside in most glass frogs, the color of the bones also helps to tell some species apart. The bones in the Pichincha glass frog, Pacific giant glass frog, Ecuador Cochran frog, and many others, are green. In the Atrato glass frog, Fleischmann's glass frog, and La Palma glass frog, among others, the bones are white.

The typical glass frog has a delicate body that looks as if it would easily break if handled. These slender, and often very smooth, bodies have thin front and rear legs. Some species, like the grainy Cochran frog, have hundreds of tiny bumps on their heads and backs. All of their toe bones are T-shaped at the ends. On the outside, the toes are tipped with wide, rounded pads. Thin, transparent webs stretch between their toes.

The head in the average glass frog has large bulging eyes that face mostly forward rather than to the sides and are located more toward the top of the head than the eyes in most other frogs. In many frog species, the head blends into the body and does not appear to have a neck between the head and body. The typical glass frog's head, on the other hand, is obvious, even looking round when viewed from above.

Most members of this family are small, reaching 0.7 to 1.2 inches (1.8 to 3 centimeters) from the tip of the snout to the end of the rump. Males in many species are smaller than females. In the Pichincha glass frog, for example, females grow to 1.3 inches (3.23 centimeters) long, while males reach 1.1 to 1.2 inches (2.68 to 3.15 centimeters) in length. The Nicaragua glass frog is similar. The female in this species reaches 1.0 to 1.1 inches (2.54 to 2.68 centimeters) long, while the male grows to 0.9 to 1.1 inches (2.17 to 2.68 centimeters) in length. In other species, like the Ecuador Cochran frog, the males are the larger of the two. Female Ecuador Cochran frogs reach 0.8 to 1.0 inches (2 to 2.54 centimeters) in length, while males can grow to 1.9 inches (4.83 centimeters) long. The Pacific giant glass frog is truly a giant among glass frogs. Although not large when compared to frogs in some other families, the male's 3.2-inch (8.13-centimeter) body makes it the biggest of the glass frogs. Female Pacific giant glass frogs are not quite as large, but they are still giants compared to most other glass frogs. Females can reach 2.4 to 2.9 inches (6.09 to 7.36 centimeters) in length.

GEOGRAPHIC RANGE

Glass frogs can be found in North, Central, and South America. In North America, they only live in southern Mexico. Many species are found throughout Central America and in many parts of South America as far south as southern Brazil and northern Argentina.

HABITAT

Glass frogs are mainly land species that live in humid mountain forests. Lower on the mountains where the weather is warm, these forests are called rainforests. In colder areas higher up mountainsides, they are called cloud forests. Both areas get a good deal of rain and are very humid. Most of the glass frogs live among trees and plants that line streams. Their tadpoles live and grow in slow-moving waters of the streams. The Pichincha glass frog, for instance, lives in cloud forests high on mountains that are 6,430 to 7,870 feet (1,960 to 2,400 meters) above sea level. The Nicaraguan glass frog chooses humid forests that are not so far up. It lives about 328 to 4,921 feet (100 to 1,500 meters) above sea level. Fleischmann's glass frog goes even lower on mountainsides, down to 200 feet (60 meters) above sea level, but also may live as high as 4,790 feet (1,460 meters) above sea level. Each of these three species makes its home in plants and trees around streams.

Some people think that a few species of glass frogs, especially those that survive in Mexico, may be able to make their homes in places away from streams by living in wet plants, like bromeliads (broh-MEE-lee-ads) that grow on the sides of trees. Bromeliads often have overlapping leaves that form cups and can hold rainwater. If the water is deep enough and does not drain out or dry up, the tadpoles might be able to survive there and develop into froglets. So far, however, the tadpoles of only one species, known by its scientific name of *Centrolene buckleyi*, has been found living in a bromeliad.

DIET

Although little research has been done on their food habits, scientists think these small frogs probably mainly eat tiny insects. The large Pacific giant glass frog, however, can and does consume larger prey, including fishes and other frogs.

BEHAVIOR AND REPRODUCTION

Glass frogs are usually active at night. This, combined with their transparent bodies, makes them very difficult to spot for people or for predators. A flashlight shown on a glass frog at night reveals little of the frog except its large eyes and a dark smudge where the skull is. During the daylight, the frogs hide among the leaves. Since the rainforest and cloud forests are so full of plants and trees, the tiny green frogs can easily stay out of sight if they sit on a leaf and do not move. The frogs also become even more invisible because they squat their bodies down flat on the leaves. Even from the side, they look much like a slight lump on the leaf rather than a living frog. Only the most careful observers see the frog during the day or at night.

Because they are so well-hidden, most of the information about the glass frogs comes from studies done when the frogs are most noticeable. This happens when they breed. Some species that live in areas where the weather is about the same all year will mate on any night. Others that live in places with changing weather usually mate only at certain times. Like the Nicaraguan glass frogs, which live in Nicaragua, Costa Rica, Panama, Colombia, and Ecuador, they may mate only on nights following heavy rains.

The males of many glass frogs are fussy about the places where they want to mate and have their young. Once they find a good spot, they will often fight other males who try to take it from them. These "good spots" are known as territories. Male Nicaraguan glass frogs set up and defend the territories they will use as calling sites. Like the males of most other species of frogs, male glass frogs call to attract females for mating. In this species, two males may fight over a leaf by grasping onto a side of the leaf or a stem with their back feet, hanging upside down, and wrestling one another. The winner is the one that can knock the other off, or that can manage to scramble onto the leaf's surface and flatten down his body on it. In the Ecuador Cochran frog, males battle, again while hanging upside down but in a belly-to-belly position and with their front legs wrapped around one another's neck. They then pump their hind legs, which causes the wrestling pair to swing up and down and back and forth.

The males of many species have one sharp bony spine on the upper part of each front leg. The bone in this part of the leg is called the humerus (HYOO-mer-us). In a human, the humerus is the long bone in the arm that runs from the shoulder to the elbow. Because the spine is on the humerus, it is called a humeral (HYOO-mer-ul) spine. Males of these glass frog species often have scars on their faces, the backs of the head, and sides of the body, which suggests that the males use their humeral spines when fighting one another. For example,

NEW GLASS FROGS

People are still discovering new species of frogs, including glass frogs. In 2004, for instance, researchers from the University of Kansas announced a new species from northwestern Ecuador. In 2003, scientists from the University of Texas described a new species from western Guyana. Both of these species are green with tiny yellow dots.

the male Pacific giant glass frogs have powerful and thick front legs, unlike most other glass frogs, and long pointed humeral spines. Although no one has every seen the males of this species fighting, many males have numerous scars that match the marks that would be made if other males had sliced them with their spines. The males of many other species of glass frogs have humeral spines, too. In fact, all species that fall into one group, called the genus *Centrolene*, have humeral spines. This includes the Pacific giant glass frog, the Nicaraguan glass frog, and the Pichincha glass frog, among others. In species like the Pacific giant glass frog and the Nicaraguan glass frog, the humeral spines are sharp, but in other species, like the Pichincha glass frog, the spines have dull tips.

Males of different species have different calls, but most are some type of a whistling sound. Male Fleischmann's glass frogs call with a short trill that they repeat again and again. Male La Palma glass frogs also have a short call, but it does not trill like that of the Fleischmann's glass frog. The male Nicaraguan glass frog's call is made up of three short beeps. They may make this call as often as forty-three times an hour or as little as just once in an hour. Most males call at night and from leaves in plants or trees above streams. Some males, like the Ecuador Cochran frog, prefer spots over streams that are rushing downhill. Male Pacific giant glass frogs make their loud, trilled calls from behind waterfalls or on boulders in fast waters.

When a male glass frog attracts a female with his call and she approaches him, he climbs onto her back. This piggyback position is called amplexus (am-PLEK-sus). The male wraps his front legs around her and hangs on just behind her front legs. He remains there until she lays her eggs. As she does, he releases a fluid containing microscopic cells, called sperm, that trigger the eggs to start growing.

Usually, glass frogs mate at or near the place where the male was calling. This is the case with the Ecuador Cochran frog. She lays her eggs on the tip of the same or a nearby leaf where the male was calling. In a few species, like the Nicaraguan glass frog, the male may lead the female away from his calling site and to another place where they actually mate. In this species, the female lays her eggs on the top of a leaf near the ground on in a plant up to 10 feet (3 meters) above the ground. Sometimes, she will instead lay her eggs on mossy rocks or branches. While they are mating and even for a short time after she lays her eggs, the male continues to call. The vast majority of species in this family lay their sticky eggs either on top of or on the bottom of leaves. The Ecuador Cochran frog is one species that lays eggs on the tops of leaves. Some of the species that lay their eggs on the bottom surfaces of leaves include the Atrato glass frog and the Fleischmann's glass frog. The only member of this family that does not follow this pattern of laying eggs on leaves is the Pacific giant glass frog. This species mates in the male's calling site, which is on a wet, splashed rock behind a waterfall or sticking up next to rapids.

AN OUT-OF-THE-WAY SPOT

The glass frog, known only by its scientific name *Cochranella saxiscandens*, makes its home in what was once an out-of-the-way spot: the stream at the bottom of a steep gorge in the mountains of northern Peru. People, however, have discovered the area and have begun cutting down the nearby forests for farms and for wood.

The typical number of eggs laid by a female glass frog is about two or three dozen. Female Fleischmann's glass frogs, for instance, lay about eighteen to thirty eggs, the Nicaraguan glass frog lays about twenty, and the Atrato glass frog lays twenty to twenty-five eggs in a clutch. Eggs come in different colors, depending on the species. Some, like the Nicaraguan glass frogs, have black eggs, while others, like the Atrato glass frog, lay transparent green eggs.

It is common to see an adult staying with the eggs for at least a short time. The female Nicaraguan frog stays with her clutch for at least the first night. In the Atrato glass frog, one of the adults either sits next to or on top of the eggs. In the Fleischmann's glass frog, it is usually the male that stays with the clutch. He sits nearby during the day, but covers them with his body at night. Despite his care, fruit flies often manage to land on the frog eggs and lay their eggs on them. The fly eggs hatch into maggots that eat the frog eggs, sometimes destroying almost all of them. In La Palma glass frogs, the males are the caregivers. A male will stay with his young day in and day out. Interestingly, the pattern on the adult frog's back looks very much like the pile of eggs and may confuse predators enough to cause them to leave alone both the male and his eggs.

Glass frog eggs hatch into tadpoles, which usually slide off the leaves and drop into the water below. Sometimes, a tadpole may slide off in the wrong direction and wind up on the shore instead of in the water. Fortunately, most tadpoles have strong tails that are powerful enough to flip them into the stream. The typical tadpole is long and thin with eyes on the top of its head. In Fleischmann's glass frogs, the tadpoles are bright red in color. The red is not, however, the color of the skin. It is the color of the tadpole's blood, which shows through the skin. Once a glass frog's eggs hatch into tadpoles, the adult leaves the clutch, and the tadpoles continue their development, eventually turning into froglets, on their own.

GLASS FROGS AND PEOPLE

People rarely see glass frogs in the wild or in the pet trade. Conservationists are especially interested in these little frogs because they may be good bioindicators (bie-oh-IN-dih-KAY-torz). A bioindicator is a living thing that provides clues about the health of the place where it lives. Glass frogs live in rainforests and cloud forests that are affected by global warming. As the Earth's weather changes, some of these forests are becoming too dry and making life difficult for the frogs, as well as other plants and animals. By watching the frogs, scientists can learn how much of a problem global warming might cause.

CONSERVATION STATUS

Of the 134 species in this family, the World Conservation Union (IUCN) considers sixty to be at risk, and another forty-nine to be Data Deficient, which means too little information is available to make a judgment about the threat of extinction. Of the sixty at-risk species, six are Critically Endangered and face an extremely high risk of extinction in the wild. These include *Centrolene ballux, Centrolene gemmatum, Centrolene heloderma, Centrolene puyoense, Cochranella anomala,* and *Hyalinobatrachium crybetes.* Many of the glass frogs are little known and have no common names in the English language. Two of these, *Centrolene ballux* and *Centrolene heloderma,* have lost eighty percent of their total number in a very short time. *Centrolene ballux,* which lives in Colombia and Ecuador, has become very rare in both countries and has not been seen at all in Ecuador since 1989. *Centrolene heloderma* also lives in Ecuador and Colombia, but has not been seen in Ecuador since

1979. The disappearance of both frogs may be tied to global warming. As the temperatures have changed, the sky is no longer as cloudy as it once was in the frog's habitat. Without the clouds, the weather may be becoming too dry for the frogs. In addition, people are cutting down the frog's forests to build homes, create farms, or to take the logs, and fires are also destroying the forest.

The other four Critically Endangered glass frogs live in very small areas. One makes its home in Honduras, and the other three in Ecuador. In each case, the frog's forest has been destroyed for purposes as farming or logging. The forests where the only known population of *Centrolene puyoense* lived, for example, was cut down and the land cleared out in 1996.

Besides the Critically Endangered species, sixteen are Endangered and face a very high risk of extinction in the wild, twenty-nine are Vulnerable and face a high risk of extinction in the wild, and nine are Near Threatened and at risk of becoming threatened with extinction in the future. Habitat loss and possibly infection with a fungus, called chytrid (KIT-rid) fungus, are likely causing many of the problems for these frogs. Others appear to be quite rare, but scientists are unsure about how many individuals actually live in the wild. The glass frogs are difficult to spot at night when they are active and during the day when they sit still on leaves. In addition, many of the species spend almost all of their time high up in trees and other hard-to-reach spots. An example is the species known by its scientific name of *Cochranella luminosa*. This glass frog is found on the western side of the Andes Mountains in Colombia, where it lives at the tops of trees. Recently, however, scientists have begun studying the tops of trees, called a forest's canopy (CAN-oh-pee), using ropes and tall platforms. With these new methods, they will likely learn much more about tree-living frogs, as well as other species of plants and animals.

Lynch's Cochran frog (*Cochranella ignota*)

LYNCH'S COCHRAN FROG
Cochranella ignota

Physical characteristics: Unlike most glass frogs, Lynch's Cochran frog is not green. This small frog is usually tan, although it is sometimes greenish brown, and has small, orange- or yellow-centered black spots on its back, head, and legs. Its body and all four legs are thin. The back legs are quite long and have webbed toes. The toes on both the front and back legs end in large, round pads. Its skin is smooth, except for numerous low, white warts. Its head has very large eyes pointed toward the front and a wide, rounded snout. Its bones are light green. Females are usually about an inch (2.42 to 2.44 centimeters) long from snout to rump. Males grow to 0.9 to 1.0 inches (2.23 to 2.54 centimeters) in length.

Geographic range: Lynch's Cochran frog lives in the western Andes Mountains of Colombia.

Habitat: This frog makes its home around streams in mountain cloud forests from 6,230 to 6,430 feet (1,900 to 1,960 meters) above sea level.

Diet: Its diet is unknown.

Behavior and reproduction: Scientists know little about its behavior, but if it is like many other glass frogs, it probably hides in plants during the day and becomes active at night. To mate, the males attract females with their call, which is a repeated chirping sound. The males call from plants above streams.

Lynch's Cochran frogs and people: Few people have ever seen this frog.

Conservation status: The World Conservation Union (IUCN) lists this frog as Near Threatened, which means that it is at risk of becoming threatened with extinction in the future. This is a common species, but it lives in a small area. Fortunately, most of the area falls within national parks, where the land is protected. Conservationists are still concerned that global warming may affect the future of this frog. A warmer climate may cause weather that is too dry for this species. ∎

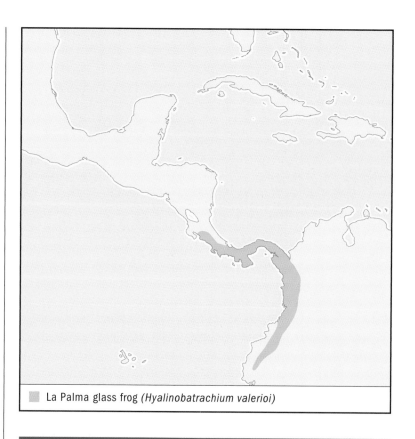

■ La Palma glass frog *(Hyalinobatrachium valerioi)*

LA PALMA GLASS FROG
Hyalinobatrachium valerioi

Physical characteristics: Also known as the reticulated glass frog, the La Palma glass frog's head and smooth back are yellow or slightly orange yellow with a net pattern that is green with dark spots. The net pattern forms a series of circles. Looked at another way, the back appears green with large yellow to slightly orange yellow spots. The legs have the same colors and pattern, and the hind legs are especially long and thin. The toes, which are almost completely transparent, have some webbing. Unlike the smooth back, the belly and the thighs are slightly wrinkly. Its bones are white. Males grow to 0.8 to 1.0 inches (2.03 to 2.54 centimeters) from snout to rump. Females are about the same size.

Geographic range: The La Palma glass frog lives in Costa Rica and Panama in Central America and in Ecuador and Colombia in South America.

Of all the glass frogs, most of which care for their eggs, the male La Palma glass frog spends the most time with his young. (Illustration by Emily Damstra. Reproduced by permission.)

Habitat: According to the IUCN, it lives in lowland forests below 1,312 feet (400 meters) above sea level, especially in plants and trees that line streams.

Diet: Its diet is unknown.

Behavior and reproduction: Scientists know little about its behavior outside of its breeding, but if the La Palma glass frog is like many other glass frogs, it probably hides in plants during the day and becomes active at night. To mate, the male calls in females with a short "seet" whistle that it repeats again and again. Males and females mate, and the females lay their eggs on leaves above streams. The eggs, which may number about three dozen, are pale green and surrounded with gel. After she lays her eggs, the female leaves, but the male stays behind to provide 24-hour-a-day protection to the eggs. Of all the glass frogs, most of which care for their eggs, the male La Palma glass frog spends the most time with his young. The color and pattern on the male's back looks very much like the clump of eggs he guards. This may confuse predators and cause them to leave both the adult male and the eggs alone.

La Palma glass frogs and people: Few people have ever seen this frog.

Conservation status: The IUCN lists this species as being of Least Concern, which means there is no known threat of extinction and the animal does not qualify for any of the "threatened" categories.

The La Palma glass frog lives over a large area and seems to be doing quite well, but conservationists are still watching it carefully. Parts of its forests are disappearing to farming, logging, and land for building, and this may eventually cause problems for the frog. Some of its forest home lies within protected areas, which are off limits to tree-cutting. ■

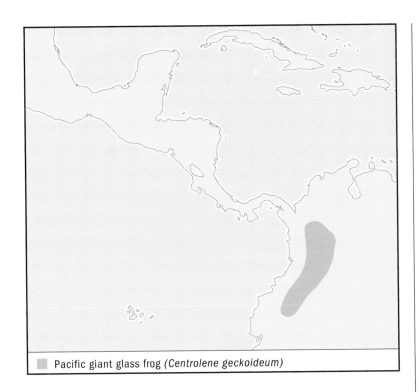

Pacific giant glass frog (*Centrolene geckoideum*)

PACIFIC GIANT GLASS FROG
Centrolene geckoideum

Physical characteristics: The Pacific giant glass frog is the largest species in this family. The typical glass frog is about an inch (2.54 centimeters) long from snout to rump, but the Pacific giant glass frog is about three times as large. Females can reach 2.4 to 2.9 inches (6.09 to 7.36 centimeters) in length, while males can grow to 2.8 to 3.2 inches (7.1 to 8.1 centimeters) long. The Pacific giant glass frog looks different from other glass frogs in other ways, too. Unlike other glass frogs, its eyes are small compared to the size of its head; its legs are rather short and thick; its toes are well-webbed; and its toes have large toe pads that are rectangular shaped instead of round. Pacific giant glass frogs are dark green to lime green in color, and their skin is covered with small bumps, or tubercles (TOO-ber-kulz), and a few small white specks. Their bones are green. Besides being bigger overall, males have stronger front legs than females; they have bony spines, called humeral spines, that stick out of the upper part of each front

leg, while females have no spines; and their skin tubercles have tiny spikes that the females lack. Pacific giant glass frog tadpoles are long and thin with two eyes on the top of the head.

Geographic range:　Pacific giant glass frogs live in Ecuador and Colombia.

Habitat:　They live high in mountain cloud forests from 5,740 to 9,840 feet (1,750 to 3,000 meters) above sea level. They prefer forests that shade waterfalls or rapids.

Diet:　This large species not only eats various insects, but it may also consume fishes or other frogs.

Behavior and reproduction:　Like other glass frogs, the Pacific giant glass frog is active at night. But unlike the others, it may spend its days not only among leaves as other members of this family do, but on rocks. It also uses rocks rather than plants when it mates. The male Pacific giant glass frog hops onto wet rocks that are splashed by water from waterfalls or rapids. From there, it makes its call to attract females. The call is a high trill that is loud enough to be heard over the crashing water. It repeats its call every 1.5 to 5 seconds. Many of the male Pacific giant glass frogs have scars on their faces, heads, and sides. Scientists think the scars are the result of injuries suffered when males use their sharp arm spines to fight one another over the places where they call or where they mate. This is just a guess, however, because no one has seen the frogs fighting in this way.

Pacific giant glass frogs and people: Few people have ever seen this frog.

Conservation status: The World Conservation Union (IUCN) lists this species as Vulnerable, which means that it is facing a high risk of extinction in the wild. It already lives in a fairly small area of forests, much of which has already had parts cut down and cleared for farming. More habitat loss will likely occur. Besides the threat from habitat destruction, the frog is also in danger from fishes that have been introduced to the streams where its tadpoles live. The fishes eat tadpoles. In addition, some people have planted illegal crops in land near the forests where the frogs live and spray the crops with chemicals that are dangerous to the frogs. Rain washes the chemicals into the streams, and this can harm the tadpoles. These threats led the IUCN to predict in 2004 that the number of Pacific giant glass frogs would drop by another thirty percent by the year 2014. ■

FOR MORE INFORMATION

Books:

Beletsky, Les. *Costa Rica: The Ecotraveller's Wildlife Guide.* San Diego, CA: Academic Press, 1998.

Cogger, Harold G., and Richard G. Zweifel. *Encyclopedia of Reptiles and Amphibians.* San Diego, CA: Academic Press, 1998.

Halliday, Tim, and Kraig Adler, eds. *The Encyclopedia of Reptiles and Amphibians (Smithsonian Handbooks).* New York: Facts on File, 1991.

Lovett, Sarah. *Extremely Weird Frogs.* Santa Fe, NM: John Muir Publications, 1996.

Mattison, Chris. *Frogs and Toads of the World.* New York: Facts on File Publications, 1987.

Meyer, John R., and Carol F. Foster. *A Guide to the Frogs and Toads of Belize.* Malabar, FL: Krieger Publishing Co., 1996.

Showler, Dave. *Frogs and Toads: A Golden Guide.* New York: St. Martin's Press, 2004.

Web sites:

Cannatella, David. "Centrolenidae." *Texas Memorial Museum, University of Texas.* http://www.zo.utexas.edu/research/salientia/centrolenidae/centrolenidae.html (accessed on April 19, 2005).

"Emerald Glass Frog." *WildHerps.* http://www.wildherps.com/species/C.prosoblepon.html (accessed on April 19, 2005).

"Family Centrolenidae." *Animal Diversity Web.* http://animaldiversity.ummz.umich.edu/site/accounts/classification/Centrolenidae.html (accessed on April 19, 2005).

Heying, H. "Centrolenidae." *Animal Diversity Web.* http://animaldiversity.ummz.umich.edu/site/accounts/information/Centrolenidae.html (accessed on April 19, 2005).

Kubicki, Brian. "Chiriqui Glass Frog." *Herps of Panama.* http://home.earthlink.net/%7Eitec1/Anura/Centronella/Hyalinobatrachium_pulvertum.html (accessed on April 19, 2005).

Kubicki, Brian. "La Palma Glass Frog." *Herps of Panama.* http://home.earthlink.net/%7Eitec1/Anura/Centronella/Hyalinobatrachium_valerioi.html (accessed on April 19, 2005).

Kubicki, Brian. "White-spotted Cochran Frog." *Herps of Panama.* http://home.earthlink.net/%7Eitec1/Anura/Centronella/Cochranella_albomaculata.html (accessed on April 19, 2005).

**AMERO-AUSTRALIAN
TREEFROGS**

Hylidae

Class: Amphibia

Order: Anura

Family: Hylidae

Number of species: 854 species

family

CHAPTER

phylum

class

subclass

order

monotypic order

suborder

▲ **family**

PHYSICAL CHARACTERISTICS

The many species of Amero-Australian treefrogs often appear very different from one another. Inside their bodies, however, they have similar skeletons. For example, the set of bones on one side of the chest overlaps with the set on the other side, and the bones at the tips of the toes are shaped like claws. From the outside, most of the treefrogs have slender bodies, long legs, and wide toe pads that may be round or triangular-shaped. A few of them have plump bodies and short legs, and some have no toe pads. Most have webs that reach at least halfway up their rear toes. Webbing on the front toes is present in some species, but not in others.

All of the Amero-Australian treefrogs have teeth on the top of the mouth. Only a few have teeth or teethlike bones on the bottom of the mouth. Most have a round eardrum that shows on each side of the head. Some have smooth, shiny skin, but others are covered with small bumps. A few, like the horned treefrog, have large heads, small spikes above their eyes, and two large points on the top of the head that might be mistaken for ears or horns.

Most of the frogs in this family are green or brown with dark markings. These camouflage colors and patterns help them to blend in with their surroundings. Their undersides are typically light in color, sometimes with light brown, brown, or black marks. Many have bright patches on their sides and/or the insides of the hind legs. The red-eyed treefrog, for example, is a lime green frog with sides that are each colored with a set of large blue areas separated by thin white to yellowish lines. A few treefrogs, such as the Chachi treefrog, are very colorful on their backs, too. This frog is yellow with a detailed pattern of red to reddish brown on its back and head.

Depending on the species, Amero-Australian treefrogs may be as small as 0.8 inches (2 centimeters) from the tip of the snout to the end of the rump or as large as 4.8 inches (2 to 12 centimeters). Males usually look similar to females, but commonly are smaller and may have bright yellow or dark gray vocal sacs. In addition, most males have rough patches and occasionally spines that form on their front legs and/or feet during the breeding season. These patches are called nuptial (NUHP-shul) pads and help the male hold onto the female during mating.

GEOGRAPHIC RANGE

Amero-Australian treefrogs live in much of North, South, and Central America, Europe, eastern and parts of southeastern Asia, Australia, and far northern Africa. They are not found in the northern reaches of North America, where the weather is frigid, nor in extreme southern South America.

HABITAT

Most Amero-Australian treefrogs live in rainforests or in other warm, moist forests. Some rainforests around the Amazon River in South America are home to more than 40 different species from this family. Numerous other species, however, live in cooler areas like the forests of the northern United States and Canada. Some treefrogs prefer drier spots, such as grassy fields and even deserts. The majority of treefrogs live up to their name and live in trees or at least on plants. Some, especially those that live in dry areas, may live on the ground or underground.

DIET

Amero-Australian treefrogs hunt by ambush, which means that they sit still, wait for a creature to wander by, and then quickly nab it and eat it. The majority of the treefrogs eat only arthropods (AR-throe-pawds), which are insects, spiders, and other animals that have no backbones, but have jointed legs. An animal without a backbone is called an invertebrate (in-VER-teh-breht). A few treefrogs are especially picky eaters. The greater hatchet-faced treefrog, for instance, is a small, green frog that usually only eats ants. Some of the treefrogs, such as the Sumaco horned treefrog, have large heads and large mouths and are able to grab and swallow larger animals, including small lizards and frogs.

BEHAVIOR AND REPRODUCTION

Almost all of the treefrogs are active at night and hide during the daytime. Their hiding places may be underneath loose bark on the side of a tree, between two leaves or between a leaf and a stem, in a crack in a rock, or tucked into any number of other tiny openings. A few species, including the northern cricket frog of North America, are active during the day instead. Those that are active at night spend most of the time sitting still on leaves or branches, or on the ground, waiting for a meal to wander past. People usually see them most often during or after a rain when the frogs move around more.

The treefrogs that live in deserts and grassy fields take special steps to keep from drying out. The water-holding frog of Australia lives in very dry parts of Australia. To survive, it spends most of its life underground. Like other burrowing treefrogs, it has shovel-like bumps, called tubercles (TOO-ber-kulz), on its feet to help it dig backward into the ground. Once it is completely buried, it sheds its skin, which hardens into a waterproof coat. The frog remains inside the coat until the rainy season arrives, and then comes out of its burrow to mate and to eat until the dry weather returns. This resting period is called estivation (es-tih-VAY-shun). Some treefrogs in hot places in South America can survive above the ground. They ooze a goop from their skin and smear it on the rest of the body. The goop is waxy and prevents the frog from drying up.

Frogs that live in cold climates, such as the northern United States and Canada, spend the winter in a state of deep sleep. This is called hibernation (high-bur-NAY-shun). Cope's gray treefrog is an example. It crawls into a hiding place under leaves or underground and stays there until spring. During hibernation, much of the frog's body freezes solid, but the frog thaws out safely when the weather starts to warm up.

The typical treefrog avoids many of its predators by staying out of sight during the daytime and by remaining still for most of the night and blending into its surroundings. If a predator spots a treefrog and draws near, most treefrogs are good jumpers and will simply leap away. A few, like the black-eyed leaf frog,

TWIN FROGS

Two of the treefrogs that live in the forests of North America are able to change colors from a bright grass green to a brown-and-black, tree bark pattern—or vice versa—in a matter of about an hour. The two frogs, known as the eastern gray treefrog and Cope's gray treefrog, not only have the same color-changing ability, but they also look almost identical. Even frog experts often cannot tell one from the other unless they hear them. The males of both species make a trilling call, but when they are calling at the same time, the call of the male Cope's gray treefrog is noticeably faster.

can soar many feet (several meters) after leaping from a high branch. Others, such as the northern cricket frog, can hop to the water and continue scooting across the surface for a short distance. Some species of Amero-Australian treefrogs do not try to leap away and instead play dead by tucking their legs against the body and freezing in that position. Often a predator will lose interest and wander away, leaving the frog alive. The Amazonian milk frog and several other treefrogs have another way to avoid predators. These frogs ooze a milky substance from the skin that hurts the eyes and mouth of a predator.

Breeding season for the frogs that live in moist forests, such as cloud forests in the mountains or rainforests, may continue off and on throughout year after almost any heavy rain. These frogs usually mate in streams or ponds that are filled with water all year long. The frogs that live in cooler climates typically breed in the spring and use temporary pools of water that will dry up later in the year. Treefrogs that live in dry areas also use temporary pools, but they breed only when the rainy season arrives, which sometimes does not happen for a year, two years, or more. While many other species of treefrogs will call and mate in large groups, the males of those species that breed on land usually call alone. For example, a male spiny-headed treefrog calls alone from a tree hole or from a bromeliad (broh-MEE-lee-ad), which is a plant that grows on trees and holds little puddles of water between its leaves. When the male pairs with a female, the two also mate away from the other frogs.

The males' calls announce the breeding season. The males usually have a single vocal sac, a bit of flesh on the throat area that blows up and deflates when they call. Most call from the ground or on plants or trees. A few species, like the Manaus slender-legged treefrog, have two vocal sacs that inflate upward around the head, and they call while floating in the water. If they had the typical single vocal sac that inflates out and down from the throat, they would bob around in the water. In most species, the male finds a good spot for breeding and makes his calls not only to attract a female but also to announce his territory to other males of his species. If another male tries to move into his territory despite his calls, the two may wrestle with one another, sometimes even resorting to biting. Perhaps the most vicious fighters are the male gladiator frogs, which have sharp spines on the inner toe of each front foot. Two battling males will swipe their spines at each other, often causing bad cuts and sometimes death. Spiny-headed treefrogs may also fight by gashing one another with their head spines.

Once a female approaches a male for mating, he scrambles up and lays flat against her back while hanging on with his front legs wrapped around the top of her back. The females of some treefrogs, including many of the species in North America, lay their eggs in the water, and the eggs hatch into tadpoles. Some treefrogs instead dig a shallow dip or a deeper hole in the ground or find an already-made dip and lay their eggs there. When rain floods the dip or the burrow, the tadpoles hatch and float off to a nearby pool of water. The females of other treefrog species lay their eggs on leaves that hang over the water or make foamy nests for them on plants above the water. A number of treefrog females lay their eggs on the sides of tree holes or on bromeliad leaves above a little puddle of water. These eggs hatch into tadpoles and slide off the leaves, drop out of the nests, or wriggle from the sides of bromeliad leaves and tree holes to fall into the water below. In some species of treefrogs, the eggs spend time inside a pouch on the female's back or simply stuck to her back. Among several of these species, the eggs hatch into tadpoles inside the pouch or on the female's back, and she drops them off at a pond or in a puddle inside a tree hole or bromeliad. The eggs in a few species never become tadpoles at all and hatch right into froglets.

AMERO-AUSTRALIAN TREEFROGS AND PEOPLE

Some local people in tropical areas eat the larger Amero-Australian treefrogs, including the very large tadpoles that are seen in some species. Some treefrogs, however, are not safe to eat. The giant waxy monkey treefrog, for instance, oozes a very powerful poison from its skin that can cause a person to become extremely sick or to die.

Many species of treefrogs can be found in the pet trade. The red-eyed treefrog with its green back, blue-and-white sides, orange toes, and large, red eyes is especially common.

CONSERVATION STATUS

The World Conservation Union (IUCN) lists one species that is Extinct, which means that it is no longer in existence; fifty-three species that are Critically Endangered and facing an extremely high risk of extinction in the wild; seventy-seven species that are Endangered and facing a very high risk of extinction in the wild; fifty-four that are Vulnerable and facing a high risk of extinction in the wild; twenty-seven that are Near Threatened and at risk of becoming threatened with extinction in the future; and 183 that are Data Deficient, which means that scientists do not have enough information to make a judgment about the threat of extinction.

The one Extinct species was from Brazil. Known as the spiny-knee leaf frog, the first—and only—one was seen more than eighty years ago. Scientists have looked for others since then, but have found none. Many of the fifty-three Critically Endangered species in this family have had die-offs because of infection with a fungus, called chytrid (KIT-rid) fungus. This fungus has also killed frogs from many other species in different frog families around the world. Morelet's treefrog, which is found in Central America and Mexico, is one of the species of Amero-Australian treefrogs that has had a loss in numbers because of the fungus. Some individuals have probably also died as their forests have been destroyed. This frog was once quite common, but now it has disappeared from many places. Scientists believe that its population will drop by another 80 percent by the year 2014.

Riobamba marsupial frog (*Gastrotheca riobambae*)

RIOBAMBA MARSUPIAL FROG
Gastrotheca riobambae

Physical characteristics: Also known as the Ecuadorian marsupial frog, the Riobamba marsupial frog gets its name from the pouch, or marsupium (mar-SOUP-ee-uhm), on the rear of the female's back. The male has no pouch. The Riobamba marsupial frog is a plump green to brown frog sometimes with darker colored oblong blotches of color on its back. The blotches are outlined in dark brown. Its back is smooth or has a cracked appearance. Its underside is grainy-looking, has a cream color, and is sometimes spotted with gray or brown. The frog has a small head with large, brown eyes and a wide mouth on its

rounded snout. All four of its short legs have toes with slightly rounded pads on the tips. Males may be a bit shorter than females. Males usually grow to 1.4 to 2.3 inches (3.4 to 5.7 centimeters) from snout to rump, while females reach 1.4 to 2.7 inches (3.4 to 6.6 centimeters) in length. Until 1972, this frog's scientific name was *Gastrotheca marsupiata*, but that name is now used by a different species found only in Peru and Bolivia.

Geographic range: It lives in northwestern South America among the Andes mountains in parts of Ecuador.

Habitat: It lives along the ground, making its home in mountain fields, farmlands, and even city gardens.

Diet: It eats beetles, as well as other arthropods.

Behavior and reproduction: The Riobamba marsupial frog hides during the day in small openings in rock piles and stone walls and among plant leaves. At night, it becomes active and looks for food on the ground. The frog is most known for the unusual way it has its young. Mating begins when the male calls with a "wraaack-ack-ack" sound and attracts a female. In most frogs, the male sheds fluid, which contains microscopic cells called sperm, over the female's eggs as she lays them. Only after the sperm mixes with the eggs can they start developing into baby frogs. In the Riobamba marsupial frog, the male sheds the sperm-filled fluid, but spreads it on her back behind her pouch. As she lays her eggs, he pushes them through the fluid and into her pouch. A single female may lay sixty-four to 166 eggs at a time. The eggs hatch inside her pouch seventy to 108 days later. The female moves to shallow water, pulls open the pouch, and the tadpoles swim out. The female uses her hind feet to scoop out any stragglers. The tadpoles change into froglets in four to 12 months.

Riobamba marsupial frogs and people: Scientists are interested in the frog because of the unusual way it reproduces.

Conservation status: The IUCN lists this species as Endangered, which means that it faces a very high risk of extinction in the wild. It was once a common species, but now is rare. Scientists are not sure why its numbers have dropped, but they think that the change in its habitat from forests and meadows to farm fields is likely part of the reason. ■

Sumaco horned treefrog *(Hemiphractus proboscideus)*

SUMACO HORNED TREEFROG
Hemiphractus proboscideus

Physical characteristics: The many jagged edges of the Sumaco horned treefrog set it apart from most other frogs. Its head is very large compared to its body. The snout is wide and triangular with a very pointy front. It has other edges on its head that give it the appearance of having pointy "cheeks" and "ears." Its eyes are large and set toward the side, and it has additional small points above its eyes. The Sumaco horned treefrog is several shades of brown, often with noticeable dark streaks on its face and dark bands on its legs. Its body is a bit flattened, and parts of the backbone poke up enough

With its large mouth, this frog is able to eat large arthropods, as well as small lizards and other frogs. (Illustration by Amanda Humphrey. Reproduced by permission.)

that they are visible as bumps down the middle of the back. The underside is brown and spotted with light brown or orange. It has long, thin legs and long, knobby toes. The toes on the front feet have no webs, but the toes on the back feet do have some webbing. Females are larger than males. Males reach 1.8 to 2.0 inches (4.3 to 5.0 centimeters) long, but females grow to 2.3 to 2.7 inches (5.7 to 6.6 centimeters) in length.

Geographic range: The Sumaco horned treefrog lives in northwestern South America, including parts of Ecuador, Peru, and Colombia.

Habitat: This frog can be found climbing through moist forests of lowland areas or low on mountains. It does not mate or have its young in the water.

Diet: With its large mouth, this frog is able to eat large arthropods, as well as small lizards and other frogs.

Behavior and reproduction: The Sumaco horned treefrog is active at night, when it moves through the trees of the forest. When it stays still, its body color and shape blend into the leaves. If a predator approaches, the frog will open its quite large mouth to flash its bright yellow tongue. This display may startle a predator and convince it to leave the frog be. Like the female Riobamba marsupial frog, the female Sumaco horned treefrog carries her eggs on her back, but the Sumaco horned treefrog does not have a pouch. Instead, the eggs stick to the top of her back. A typical female has about twenty-six large eggs at a time. The eggs skip the tadpole stage and hatch right into froglets.

Sumaco horned treefrogs and people: People rarely see or bother this frog.

Conservation status: The Sumaco horned treefrog is not considered endangered or threatened. ■

Hourglass treefrog (Hyla leucophyllata)

HOURGLASS TREEFROG
Hyla leucophyllata

Physical characteristics: The hourglass treefrog, which is also known as the Bereis' treefrog, is a small, slender, reddish brown frog that looks as if someone has dabbed it with streaks of cream or yellow paint. A triangle of color covers the head from one of its large eyes to the other and down onto its short, rounded snout. The color continues down each side of the smooth body, leaving a somewhat hourglass-shaped patch of brown in the middle of the back. An oblong cream or yellow patch sits on the rump, and additional rounded or oblong patches dot the front and back legs. It has long, thin legs,

and its toes are tipped in rounded pads. In some individuals, the toes are yellow. The undersides of its legs are orange, as is the slight webbing between its toes. Males are 1.3 to 1.5 inches (3.3 to 3.6 centimeters) from the snout to the rump. Females are larger at 1.6 to 1.8 inches (4.0 to 4.4 centimeters) in length.

Geographic range: This treefrog makes its home in northern South America, from northern and western Brazil through Bolivia to Peru, and also in Colombia, Ecuador, Suriname, French Guiana, and Guyana.

Habitat: It lives in hot and humid, lowland rainforests. Tadpoles develop in shallow ponds.

Diet: It mainly eats moths, but will also eat other small insects. Tadpoles swim to the pond bottom and feed on large bits of plants and other items underwater.

Behavior and reproduction: The hourglass treefrog is active at night, when it climbs through trees looking for food. To mate, a male begins calling from a spot in plants above a pond. His call may be three to eight notes long, with the first being the longest. When a female approaches, he positions himself on her back, clutching her near her front legs, and she lays her eggs. One female can lay about six hundred eggs, which she drops onto the plants. In five to seven days, the eggs hatch into tadpoles, which plop down into the water below.

Hourglass treefrogs and people: It is occasionally seen in the pet trade.

Conservation status: The IUCN does not consider this frog to be endangered or threatened.   ■

Amazonian skittering frog (*Scarthyla goinorum*)

Physical characteristics: The Amazonian skittering frog is a small and slender frog. Its head, back, and legs are light green and grainy-looking. Its head has a small, somewhat pointed snout and two large eyes, one on each side. The legs are thin, and the hind legs are long. All of its toes are webbed and have small rounded pads at the tips. Brown and white stripes run from the chin down the sides of its body. Its underside is white. Males, which grow to 0.6 to 0.8 inches (1.5 to 2.0 centimeters) long, are slightly smaller than females. Females reach 0.7 to 0.9 inches (1.8 to 2.3 centimeters) in length.

Geographic range: It lives in western South America, including far western Brazil, Bolivia, Colombia, and Peru.

Habitat: This small frog lives among the leaves of plants that stretch along and over ponds in warm and humid lowland rainforests.

Diet: It mainly eats spiders, but also eats other small arthropods.

Behavior and reproduction: Active at night, it either sits among leaves that hang low over ponds or skitters across the water. When it skitters, it scoots across the surface of the water without sinking. To attract females for mating, the male makes his whistling calls with a pattern of eight to ten notes in a row. Each female lays 130 to 202 small eggs, which she drops in the pond water. The eggs hatch into tadpoles, each of which is able to flip its strong tail and soar free of the water and through the air, sometimes eight to twelve inches at a time. Usually, however, the tadpoles stay in the water, swimming just below the surface.

Amazonian skittering frogs and people: Although it is quite common, people rarely see this frog.

Conservation status: The Amazonian skittering frog is not considered endangered or threatened. ■

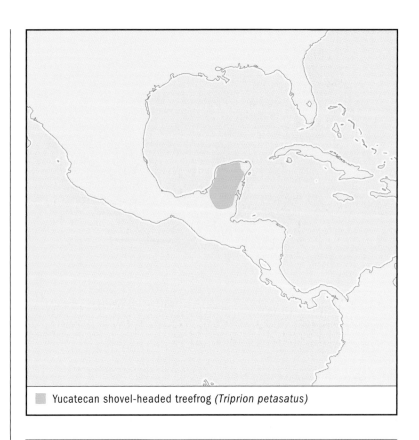

Yucatecan shovel-headed treefrog *(Triprion petasatus)*

YUCATECAN SHOVEL-HEADED TREEFROG
Triprion petasatus

Physical characteristics: The Yucatecan shovel-headed treefrog is a slender frog with a flattened head somewhat shaped like the blade of a shovel. It is sometimes called a duckbill frog or a casque (kask)-headed frog. The head has a flat outer rim on the snout and a V-shaped ridge on the top of the snout. The large, copper-colored eyes are set far apart on the sides of the head. Its hind legs are long and thin, but its front legs are strong. The toes on all four feet are widened at the tips into round pads. The front toes have little webbing, but the back toes are about two-thirds webbed. The frog is tan to dark brownish green with brown spots on its back and blotches on its legs. Its belly is white, and the bottoms of its legs are tan, sometimes with a pink tint. Females, which reach 2.6 to 3 inches (6.5 to 7.5 centimeters) long, are larger than males. Males grow to 2 to 2.5 inches (4.8 to 6.1 centimeters) in length.

Geographic range: It is found in far southern Mexico, as well as Guatemala and Belize in Central America. A small population also survives in northwestern Honduras.

Habitat: It lives in fairly dry, shrubby forests and grasslands. Eggs and tadpoles develop in pools of water that form in the rainy season.

Diet: Like many other treefrogs in this family, it eats small arthropods. It also sometimes eats other, smaller frogs.

Behavior and reproduction: It is active at night, when it moves across the ground and through shrubs and low trees, looking for things to eat. Its body color provides excellent camouflage when it sits still against the trunk of a tree. After heavy rains create small pools on the ground, all of the males hop near the pools and begin calling from land and in bushes and trees. Each male's call is a duck-like quacking sound. Together, the males sound like a whole flock of ducks. The females approach the males and mate with them, laying their eggs in clumps in the water. All of the frogs mate in about a one-week period. The eggs hatch into tadpoles that remain in the pool until they change into froglets.

Yucatecan shovel-headed treefrogs and people: It is a very common frog that is often seen near towns.

Conservation status: This frog is not considered threatened or endangered. ■

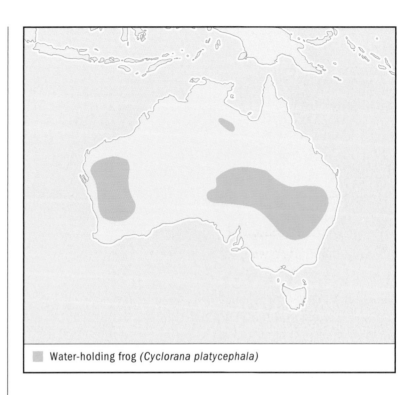

Water-holding frog (*Cyclorana platycephala*)

WATER-HOLDING FROG
Cyclorana platycephala

Physical characteristics: The water-holding frog is a chubby frog that has a round but flattened body. Its head blends into its body and does not have an obvious neck. Its eyes sit toward the top of the head. Its legs are strong, but rather short, almost disappearing under the body when the frog is sitting still. Each hind foot has a bump, or tubercle, that is shaped like the edge of a shovel blade. The toes are webbed. The frog is dark brown, gray, or green with dark blotches on its back. It usually becomes greener in the mating season. Its underside is white. Females are the larger sex. Females grow to 2.0 to 2.9 inches (5.0 to 7.2 centimeters) in length, while males reach 1.7 to 2.6 inches (4.2 to 6.4 centimeters).

Geographic range: The water-holding frog lives in three parts of Australia: a large area of the far west, a small spot in the north, and a large area in the middle of the continent from the center to the east.

The water-holding frog inflates its flexible body full of water after floods on the arid floodplain of the Paroo River, Australia. As the water recedes, the frog will burrow underground and live on its stored water. (Photograph by Wayne Lawler. Photo Researchers, Inc.)

Habitat: It spends much of its life beneath the ground of deserts and dry grasslands. During the rainy season, males and females come to the surface to mate and have their young in new, small pools of water that have filled with the rain.

Diet: It eats various arthropods that it finds during the rainy season.

Behavior and reproduction: The weather for most of the year is very dry where this frog lives, and the frog survives by digging with its hind feet and tubercles and burrowing backward into the soil to bury itself. Once dug in, sometimes as much as 3.3 feet (1 meter) deep, it sheds a few layers of skin, which harden into a cocoon that keeps its body from drying out. The frog enters a deep resting stage, called estivation, and remains in that state until the rainy season begins. In some years, even the rainy season is not wet enough, and the frogs stay underground for the entire year to wait for the next heavy rains.

When the rains fall hard enough to make shallow pools on the ground, the frogs crawl out from underground. The males call with long, snore-like sounds. Females find the males and mate with them. Each female lays clumps of eggs—sometimes several hundred—in the pools. The eggs hatch into tadpoles, which must turn into frogs before the pools dry up. This can take as little as thirty days. As the rainy season ends, the frogs fill their bodies with water before digging back underground to wait for the next bout of wet weather.

Water-holding frogs and people: Native people, called Australian aborigines (ab-or-RIJ-ih-neez), live in the same area as the frogs. The people sometimes dig the animals from their underground burrows and squeeze them to get a sip of water out of the frog.

Conservation status: The water-holding frog is not considered threatened or endangered. ■

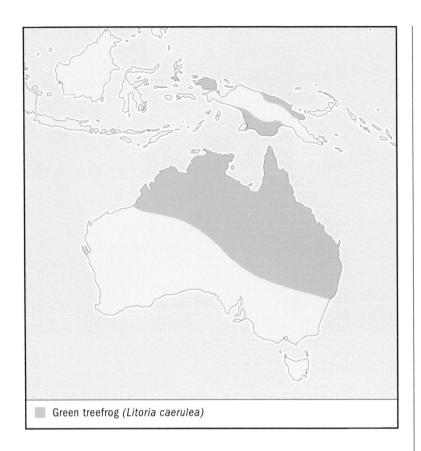

Green treefrog (*Litoria caerulea*)

Physical characteristics: The green treefrog, also known as White's treefrog, is a pudgy animal with skin that drapes over its sides to make the frog appear almost as if it were melting. The flabby-looking skin behind each side of the back of the head covers large, flat, poison glands. The green treefrog is a round frog with a head that blends back into the body rather than having an obvious neck. Its head has large, white eyes, a short snout, and a wide mouth. Its eardrums are visible on the sides of its head. Its legs are rather short, but its webbed toes are thick and long, ending in wide, triangular-shaped pads. The typical green treefrog is the color of a lime, sometimes with a tinge of yellow on its face and legs. It has a grayish or yellowish white underside. Females, which grow to 2.9 to 4.5 inches (7.0 to 11.0 centimeters) long, are

larger than males. Males reach 2.7 to 3.1 inches (6.6 to 7.7 centimeters) in length. Sometimes this frog is listed with the scientific name *Pelodryas caerulea* instead of the name listed here.

Geographic range: It lives in northern and eastern Australia and has also been introduced to New Zealand.

Habitat: It spends most of its life in the trees of forests, which may be dry or humid. Eggs and tadpoles develop in the calm water of swamps or slow streams.

Diet: This rather large frog eats various arthropods, as well as larger organisms, such as other frogs and even small mammals.

Behavior and reproduction: It often sits in trees with its front feet crossed and held close to its body. It becomes active at night. Following rains, usually from November until February or March, the males begin calling with a deep, repeated "crawk" or barking sound. They call from spots near the water. Females follow the calls to the males and they mate. The females may lay as few as two hundred eggs or ten times that many, dropping them onto the surface of calm water. The eggs soon sink and later hatch into tadpoles. The tadpoles turn into froglets in about six weeks.

Green treefrogs and people: The skin of this frog oozes a substance that can help control high blood pressure in people. High blood pressure, which happens when the blood moves with too much force through the blood vessels in the body, is a dangerous condition. Scientists now make the frog's skin substance in laboratories as a human drug.

Conservation status: The green treefrog is not considered threatened or endangered. ■

Paradox frog (*Pseudis paradoxa*)

PARADOX FROG
Pseudis paradoxa

Physical characteristics: The paradox frog, also known as the paradoxical frog, has large, bulging eyes on the top of its head and a rounded and somewhat pointed snout. It has long and powerful hind legs and shorter but still strong front legs. Its toes are webbed. Its back is light brown to greenish brown, sometimes with light-colored stripes, and its underside is white. Females grow to 1.7 to 3.2 inches (4.0 to 6.5 centimeters) from snout to rump, while males reach 1.6 to 2.7 inches (3.8 to 6.5 centimeters) in length.

Geographic range: Populations of this frog are scattered through parts of northern and central South America, from Uruguay and southern Brazil in the south to Venezuela in the north.

Habitat: It lives in grassy or open forest areas near marshes, ponds, or slow-moving creeks.

Diet: It eats water-living arthropods, as well as small frogs.

Behavior and reproduction: This frog remains in the water most of the time, often with just its eyes poking above the surface. It is mainly active at night except during its breeding season, when the males may make their loud, croaking calls at any time of night or day. Females come to the males and mate with them, laying their eggs among the plants that grow in the water. The eggs, which are grouped together in foamy clusters, hatch into tadpoles. Tadpoles continue to grow in the water and can reach lengths of 11 inches (27 centimeters) before changing into froglets. Much of the length of the tadpole is in its tail, and once that shrinks away, the froglet is much smaller.

Paradox frogs and people: Some local people eat the large tadpoles of this species.

Conservation status: The paradox frog is not considered threatened or endangered. ■

FOR MORE INFORMATION

Books:

Badger, David. *Frogs.* Stillwater, MN: Voyageur Press, 2000.

Barker, John, Gordon Grigg, and Michael J. Tyler. *A Field Guide to Australian Frogs.* Chipping Norton, Australia: Surrey Beatty and Sons, 1995.

Duellman, William E. *Hylid Frogs of Middle America.* Ithaca, NY: Society for the Study of Amphibians and Reptiles, 2001.

Halliday, Tim, and Kraig Adler, eds. *The Encyclopedia of Reptiles and Amphibians (Smithsonian Handbooks).* New York: Facts on File, 1991.

Mattison, Chris. *Frogs and Toads of the World.* New York: Facts on File Publications, 1987.

Meyer, John R., and Carol F. Foster. *A Guide to the Frogs and Toads of Belize.* Malabar, FL: Krieger Publishing Co., 1996.

Miller, Sara Swan. *Frogs and Toads: The Leggy Leapers.* New York: Franklin Watts, 2000.

Patent, Dorothy Hinshaw. *Frogs, Toads, Salamanders, and How They Reproduce.* New York: Holiday House, 1975.

Showler, Dave. *Frogs and Toads: A Golden Guide.* New York: St. Martin's Press, 2004.

Tyning, Thomas. *A Guide to Amphibians and Reptiles.* Boston, MA: Little, Brown and Company, 1990.

Periodicals:

Milius, Susan. "Wafting Pesticides Taint Far-flung Frogs." *Science News* (December 16, 2000): 391.

Milius, Susan. "Wasps Drive Frog Eggs to (Escape) Hatch." *Science News* (October 14, 2000): 246.

Turner, Pamela S. "The Extreme Team." *Odyssey* (May 2002): 26.

Web sites:

"Sticky Fingers." *American Museum of Natural History.* http://www.amnh.org/exhibitions/frogs/featured/sticky.php (accessed on April 10, 2005).

"Wax On, Wax Off." *American Museum of Natural History.* http://www.amnh.org/exhibitions/frogs/featured/waxon.php (accessed on April 10, 2005).

TRUE FROGS
Ranidae

Class: Amphibia

Order: Anura

Family: Ranidae

Number of species: 686 species

phylum

class

subclass

order

monotypic order

suborder

▲ **family**

PHYSICAL CHARACTERISTICS

With nearly seven hundred species, the true frog family is very large. As in other big families, the true frogs come in many shapes and sizes, but they do have a few common features. All have teeth along the top of the mouth. Most of them have at least some webbing between the toes of the hind feet, and some have webbing all the way to the tips of the hind toes. In many species, the females are larger than the males, but the males have longer hind legs and more webbing between their rear toes. The males typically also have thicker front legs, which they use to hold onto the females during mating.

Most true frogs are shades of greens or browns and blend in well with their surroundings. Those that live in the water, such as Roesel's green frog and Indian tiger frog, are commonly green to olive green in color, which matches well with their homes. Often, species that live in forests, like the wood frog and Beddome's Indian frog, are tan or brown like the dead leaves that cover the forest floor. Most true frogs have rather stocky bodies. The African bullfrog is especially pudgy-looking. Some, like the leopard frog and pickerel frog, have more slender bodies. Many members of this family have long and strong hind legs for leaping. This includes the leopard, pickerel, and green frogs that are found in North America, as well as many others. Some, like the large African bullfrog, have shorter hind legs.

Many of the frogs in this family have a dark, horizontal bar through the center of each eye. Some also have a dark, vertical bar through the eye. In addition, many have a noticeable eardrum on each side of the head behind the eye. In a few species, like the green frog, the size of the eardrum can help tell a male from a female. In this species, the male's eardrum is much larger than the eye, while the female's is about the same size or smaller than the eye.

Many true frogs are between 1.6 and 3.3 inches (4.1 to 8.4 centimeters) long from the tip of the snout to the end of the rump. The smallest frogs in this family, however, are 0.4 inches (1 centimeter) long. These include several tiny African species. The largest members of this family, including the goliath frog, can reach more than 12.2 inches (31 centimeters) long.

GEOGRAPHIC RANGE

True frogs live in much of the world, including most of North and Central America, the north end and parts of central South America, most of Europe and Asia, much of Africa, and Australia. Some members of the family are also found on islands in the ocean. Some populations, like those in much of Australia, were introduced to these areas by humans and previously did not live there.

HABITAT

Many species live near water, such as a pond, quiet stream, or marsh. A few, like the goliath frog, make their homes in fast-moving rivers and rapids. Other true frogs, however, spend most of their lives away from water in forests or grasslands, and only return to ponds or wetlands once a year for breeding. Of these land-living frogs, some do not return to the water at all and instead lay their eggs in moist places on land.

DIET

Most of the true frogs are active at night and eat insects and other invertebrates (in-VER-teh-brehts), which are animals without backbones. The larger members of this family have more variety in their diets and will eat tadpoles of other species and sometimes their own, as well as animals like snakes, birds, and small mammals. Some of the true frogs hop about looking for food. Others are ambush hunters, which means that they sit still and wait for an insect or other animal to walk past. With a simple flick of the tongue or grasp of the mouth, they capture the victim and eat it whole.

BEHAVIOR AND REPRODUCTION

Although most members of this family are active at night, some that live next to lakes and ponds, or in cooler areas, are out and noticeable during the daytime. They sunbathe, or bask, by sitting in a warm spot on land or, if they are in the water, by floating in the warm, top layer. Some commonly seen day-time-basking frogs in North America include the green frog and leopard frog.

Those true frogs that live in moist forests in warm climates remain active all year. Others do not. Some live in dry areas and have to find ways to survive the weather. The African bull-frog, for example, makes its home in dry regions of southern Africa. It becomes active and breeds during the rainy season, but when the ground dries out, it buries itself underground. It then sheds a few layers of skin that it wears like a watertight coat to keep its skin from losing too much water. This skin co-coon stays around its body while the frog rests during a period that is known as estivation (es-tih-VAY-shun). The frog remains in its cocoon until the next rainy season arrives.

Frogs that live in places with cold winters also enter a rest-ing period, known as hibernation (high-bur-NAY-shun). Both hibernation and estivation are long resting periods, but one hap-pens when the weather is cold, and the other when the weather is dry. The hibernating frogs typically bury themselves in the ground or in mud at the bottom of their pond or wetland and stay there until the temperatures warm the following spring. A few species, like the wood frog of North America, are able to freeze solid in the winter and recover the next spring to live another year.

Most of the species in this family avoid predators by re-stricting their activity to the dark of night or by remaining still and blending in with the background. Since many of them live near the water, they also have the option of leaping and then diving down to make a fast escape if predators come too close. A few, like the African bullfrog, will stand their ground. They will nip at predators that approach them or their young.

Most of the frogs in this family breed during one season a year. Those that live in dry areas mate during the rainy season. Oth-ers that live in climates with cold winters start their breeding seasons when warmer spring temperatures arrive. Some breed in early spring, and others in late spring. Those that live in warm,

FROG POPSICLE

The wood frog of North America survives the cold of winter by freezing solid and remaining that way until it thaws out in the spring and hops away. Most other animals would die if frozen in this way. The wood frog prepares for winter by scooting under a pile of leaves when the chilly weather arrives in the fall. Then its body starts to make a sugary substance called glucose (GLOO-cose) that acts as antifreeze in its heart and other major organs and protects them from damage. Even though its heart does not beat, and the frog does not breathe all winter long, it continues to live to face another year.

tropical areas may breed more than once a year, often following heavy rains. Often, true frogs mate together in large groups. In the wood frogs, for example, dozens of males will hop over to the water and begin calling all at once. This type of group calling is called a chorus (KOR-us). With their quacking calls, the wood frog chorus sounds something like a large group of ducks. They, like many other species of true frogs, are explosive breeders, which means that they breed over a very short period of time. All of the wood frogs in a population, for instance, may mate over just seven to fourteen days. The male true frogs may have one or two balloon-like vocal sacs in the throat area. These fill with air and deflate as the frog makes his call. Many species, like the green frog and leopard frog, have one large vocal sac. The wood frog is one of the species with two smaller vocal sacs. They typically both inflate at the same time—one on each side of its throat.

Like females of other frog species, female true frogs follow the males' calls. Different species have different calls. The green frog, for instance, has a short "gung" call, while the leopard frog's call is more of a snoring sound. In many species, including the bullfrog, males may wrestle with one another for a good calling area. Once males and females are together, one male and one female typically pair off, the male scrambles onto her back and hangs onto her while she lays her eggs. The male in most species clings to the female by gripping near her front legs. Depending on the species, the female may lay a few or many eggs. The female Penang Taylor's frog, for instance, lays five to thirteen large eggs; the female Sanderson's hook frog lays twelve to seventeen; the female African bullfrog lays three to four thousand; the female Roesel's green frog lays two to six thousand; and the bullfrog female can lay up to twenty thousand eggs. In some species, like the African bullfrog, one male may mate with more than one female.

In most species, the females lay their eggs in the water, and the eggs hatch into tadpoles. The tadpoles may turn into froglets in a few weeks or, in some cases, in a few years. Bullfrog tadpoles are an example. They can survive as tadpoles for up to four years and even hibernate just as their parents do. In a few species, like Penang Taylor's frog, the female lays her eggs in a moist place on land, and the eggs hatch right into froglets, skipping the tadpole stage. In either case, eggs typically hatch in a matter of days to weeks. In most true frogs, neither parent provides any care for the young once the eggs are laid. In others, however, the parent may remain nearby to make sure that predators do not eat the young and/or to help keep the eggs moist if they are laid on land. The female Sanderson's hook frog even returns to her eggs every night to cover them with her body. In the African bullfrog, it is the male that watches over his young. He will bite at any intruder who comes close to his eggs or tadpoles, even if the intruder is as large as a lion or a person. If the weather becomes dry very quickly and the tadpoles are trapped in a small puddle away from the main pond, he may also dig a path through the mud to the pond so the tadpoles can swim from the puddle to the deeper water of the pond, where they continue their development.

TRUE FROGS AND PEOPLE

People from many countries, including the United States, eat frog legs. The legs usually come from large true frogs, often bullfrogs that have been captured from the wild. Some Asian and African people also make frog soups and other meals out of entire frogs and tadpoles. In addition, some people in different parts of the world use certain parts of frogs as medicines.

CONSERVATION STATUS

The World Conservation Union (IUCN) lists two of the species as being Extinct, which means that they are no longer in existence; twenty species that are Critically Endangered and face an extremely high risk of extinction in the wild; fifty-nine species that are Endangered and face a very high risk of extinction in the wild; eighty-four that are Vulnerable and face a high risk of extinction in the wild; fifty-nine that are Near Threatened and at risk of becoming threatened with extinction in the future; and 132 that are Data Deficient, which means that scientists do not have enough information to make a judgment about extinction threat.

The two Extinct species are the Las Vegas leopard frog, which is also known as the Vegas Valley leopard frog, and another species known only by its scientific name of *Nannophrys guentheri*. The Las Vegas leopard frog was only found in a few places north of Las Vegas Valley in Nevada, but it has not been seen since 1942. Ecologists believe that it died off when people rerouted water from the frog's breeding areas to the growing city of Las Vegas. A few small areas with enough water still remain, but people introduced bullfrogs to those areas. Since bullfrogs eat other, smaller frogs, any remaining Las Vegas leopard frogs would probably have been gobbled up. No one has seen the other Extinct species, *Nannophrys guentheri*, since the first one was seen in Sri Lanka more than a century ago.

One of the twenty Critically Endangered true frogs is the dusky gopher frog of the United States, which is also known as the Mississippi gopher frog. Although this species once lived in parts of Louisiana, Mississippi, and Alabama, it now only survives in a small area called Glen's Pond, which is in Mississippi's Desoto National Forest. The last members of this species were seen in Alabama in 1922 and in Louisiana in 1967. In 2001 fewer than one hundred adult frogs were still alive in Glen's Pond. Ecologists mainly blame the drop in numbers on two diseases caused by fungi. One of the fungi, known as chytrid (KIT-rid) fungus, has also killed many other frogs around the world. A Gopher Frog Recovery Team is now watching over the frog and its habitat and is trying to treat the tadpoles infected with the fungus.

In addition to the at-risk true frogs noted above, the U.S. Fish and Wildlife Service also considers four to be Endangered or Threatened. These include the California red-legged frog and the Chiricahua leopard frog, which are Threatened or likely to become endangered in the near future; and the Mississippi gopher frog described above and the mountain yellow-legged frog, which are Endangered or in danger of extinction throughout all or a significant portion of their ranges.

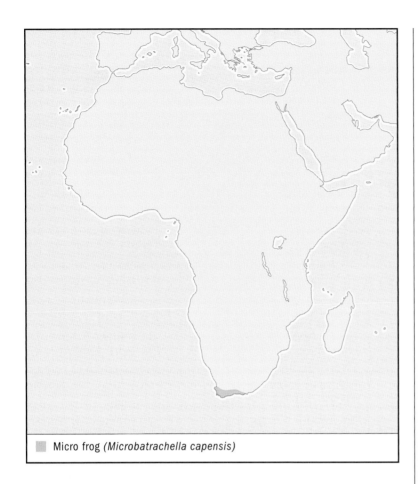

Micro frog (*Microbatrachella capensis*)

MICRO FROG
Microbatrachella capensis

Physical characteristics: As its name suggests, the micro frog is tiny. In fact, they are some of the smallest frogs in the world. Adults reach just 0.4 to 0.7 inches (1.0 to 1.8 centimeters) long from the end of the snout to the back of the rump. Their hind legs are fairly short and end in long-toed feet. The front legs are short and thin. The toes have some webbing between them, but the very long fourth toe on each rear foot is mostly free of webbing. These frogs come in several different pale or dark colors, including green, tan, reddish brown, gray, and black. A dark stripe runs from the eye to the front leg. Many frogs have a noticeable, but thin, light-colored or greenish line that starts at the snout and continues over the top of the head and down

The male and the female look very much alike. The male, however, has a large vocal sac that covers half of his underside. The vocal sac is usually not noticeable unless the male is calling. (Illustration by Jacqueline Mahannah. Reproduced by permission.)

the back to the rump. Some micro frogs also have dark patches low on their sides and dark-colored speckles on top of the back and head. The back and top of the head have a few, small, scattered warts. The underside of the frog is smooth and dappled with black and white. Sometimes the underside is pale-colored without the black-and-white pattern. The eyes are large and brownish, and the snout is short and slightly narrower toward the front. The male and the female look very much alike. The male, however, has a large vocal sac that covers half of his underside. The vocal sac is usually not noticeable unless the male is calling. To make his call, he blows up the vocal sac to a size almost as big as his entire body.

Geographic range:　The micro frog lives at the bottom of Africa in southwestern Cape Province, South Africa.

Habitat:　It makes its home in rotting plant roots of shrub-filled woodlands near small pools that fill with water only during part of the year.

Diet:　Scientists are not sure what it eats, but if it is like other small frogs in its family, it probably eats small insects or other invertebrates.

Behavior and reproduction:　Scientists know little about this frog outside of its breeding season, which runs from June to July. When they are ready to breed, the males sit in the water along the edge of the pool. There, hidden among plants that grow in the shallow water, they call with about half of their bodies above the surface. Each male calls with a one-second long scratchy noise that sounds like "tschik," which they repeat five or six times. Females follow the calls, and a male and female pair off. The female lays about twenty eggs, each of which is small and coated with gel. The eggs stick together in a clump and attach to underwater plants. The eggs hatch into tadpoles. They continue to grow in the water for the next six or seven months. In December, when they have reached about 1 inch (2.5 centimeters) long—70 percent of which is tail—they turn into baby frogs.

Micro frogs and people: People rarely see this tiny frog.

Conservation status: The IUCN considers this frog to be Critically Endangered, which means that it faces an extremely high risk of extinction in the wild. It lives in a very small area and does not do well around humans. People are, however, moving closer to the frog to construct homes and enlarge their farms. In addition, they are draining water from the wetlands where the frogs breed and have introduced new plants, which are also using up water.   ■

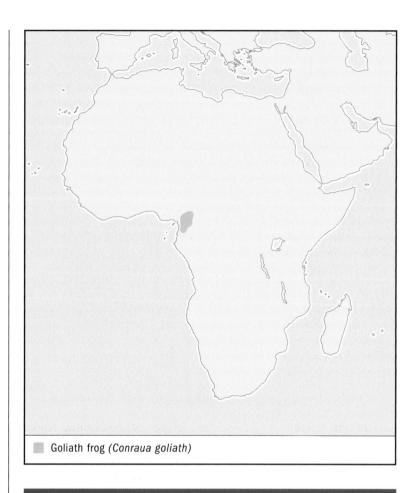

Goliath frog *(Conraua goliath)*

GOLIATH FROG
Conraua goliath

Physical characteristics: True to its name, the goliath frog is huge. It is the largest frog living on Earth today. An adult can reach a whopping 12.6 inches (32 centimeters) long from snout to rump. One frog can weigh 7 pounds (3.25 kilograms). The frog has a wide, flattened body that blends into its also-wide head without a noticeable neck. Its head is shaped like a triangle with a blunt point at the end of the snout. The frog's back, head, and the upper surface of all four legs are dark gray, sometimes a bit brownish or greenish, and covered with tiny bumps. Faint dark bars and/or spots sometimes show on the legs and lips. The underside is a lighter color, often appearing a greenish

The goliath frog is at home in rapids and other fast-moving parts of rivers. (Photograph by Paul A. Zahl. Photo Researchers, Inc.)

tan. The hind legs are long. The front legs are shorter, but thick. The toes on the front feet have a bit of webbing at their base but not out to the ends. The hind toes have full webbing all the way to their tips.

Geographic range: It lives in a small part of west-central Africa from southern Cameroon to parts of Guinea.

Habitat: The goliath frog is at home in rapids and other fast-moving parts of rivers.

Diet: Scientists are not sure what it eats. Given its enormous size, many types of food are possible.

Behavior and reproduction: Scientists know little about this frog's behavior outside of the breeding season. At that time, the males begin calling, but they do it in a way that is different than most other frogs. Most male frogs suck air into vocal sacs and blow it out to make their calls. The goliath frog and other closely related species have no vocal sacs and instead hold the mouth barely open and make a long whistling noise. Females follow the whistling to the males. One female can lay several hundred eggs at a time. Each egg is very small, about 0.14 inches (3.5 millimeters) in diameter, and sticks to plants growing in rocky areas of the river rapids. The eggs hatch into tadpoles, which can grow to 1.9 inches (4.7 centimeters) long over the next eighty-five to ninety-five days. They then turn into froglets.

Goliath frogs and people: Local people often hunt this frog for food by searching for it from boats and using a gun to shoot at it. Once they have wounded or killed it, the hunters leap into the water to snatch up the frog. New traps for capturing the frogs are making the hunters even more successful. The hunters may either eat the frogs themselves or sell them to markets. Some people also capture goliath frogs alive to sell in the pet trade, to zoos, or to people who hold frog races.

Conservation status: According to the IUCN, this species is Endangered, which means that it faces a very high risk of extinction in the wild. In the fifteen-year period from 1989 to 2004, the number of goliath frogs dropped by more than half. Hunting them for meat and collecting them for the pet trade are the main reasons for the fall in numbers. In addition, the frog's forests are also disappearing as people cut down trees, farm the land, and construct buildings. These activities are also allowing soil to run downhill and muddy up the streams where the frog breeds, and this may hurt the tadpoles. Some people believe that ecologists should begin breeding the frogs in captivity to make sure the species survives into the future. ■

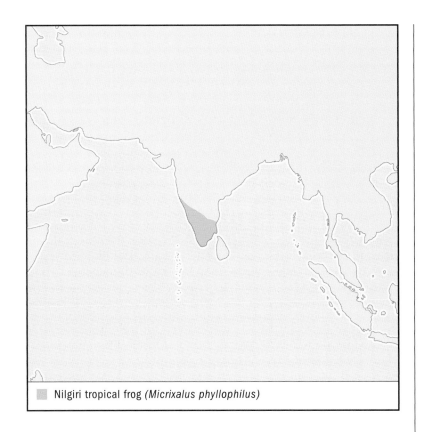

Nilgiri tropical frog (*Micrixalus phyllophilus*)

NILGIRI TROPICAL FROG
Micrixalus phyllophilus

Physical characteristics: The typical Nilgiri tropical frog is a greenish brown, smooth-skinned frog with darker patches scattered on its back and dark bands across its front and back legs. Some pink color shows on its underside beneath the legs and toward the rump. It has a ridge of skin running down each side from the snout to the rump. Its hind legs are fairly long, and their toes are fully webbed. The toes on all four feet have small, rounded tips. Males and females look much alike, except that the males develop rough pads during the mating season. Adults reach about 1.25 inches (3.175 centimeters) long from snout to rump.

Geographic range: It lives in southern India.

Habitat: The Nilgiri tropical frog makes its home in moist, humid forests on hills from about 984 to 4,593 feet (300 to 1,400 meters)

above sea level. The forests all have thick layers of dead leaves and other bits of plants lying on the ground. The frog appears to live only in forests that humans have not logged or otherwise changed.

Diet: Scientists are not sure what it eats.

Behavior and reproduction: This frog is still mostly a mystery. Other than the tadpole's appearance, scientists know little else about it. The tadpole is long with a slender tail and a mouth that opens on the bottom rather than on its front, as is the case in many other tadpoles.

Nilgiri tropical frogs and people: This frog does not survive well in disturbed forests, and people are doing just that by logging trees from woods where the frog lives.

Conservation status: The Nilgiri tropical frog is only known from one national park and two reserves, but it may live in areas between these three spots. Because the frog's home areas are small and separated from one another, and its forests are being logged, the IUCN has listed the Nilgiri tropical frog as Vulnerable, which means that it faces a high risk of extinction in the wild. It is protected by the government of India. ■

Pointed-tongue floating frog (*Occidozyga lima*)

POINTED-TONGUE FLOATING FROG
Occidozyga lima

Physical characteristics: The pointed-tongue floating frog goes by several other names, including floating spotted frog, java frog, green puddle frog, and pearly-skin puddle frog. It has a fairly plump body and a short head that narrows to a somewhat-pointed snout. It has a pointed tongue. Many small bumps cover its back, head, and legs. It is usually dark brownish green, but is sometimes pinkish brown. Some of the frogs have a thin stripe down the middle of the back. Although the webbing of their feet is thin and may be difficult to see, it is there and stretches fully between their pointy toes. Males and females look much alike, except that the males develop rough pads during the mating season. Adults reach about 1.5 inches (3.9 centimeters) long from snout to rump.

Geographic range: It lives in southeastern Asia, including southern China, India, Cambodia, Vietnam, Indonesia, and Malaysia.

The pointed-tongue floating frog goes by several other names, including floating spotted frog, java frog, green puddle frog, and pearly-skin puddle frog. (Illustration by Jacqueline Mahannah. Reproduced by permission.)

Habitat: It is believed to spend most of its time in the water of slow-moving streams, marshes, wet rice paddies, and other wetland areas. These areas are often surrounded by grasslands.

Diet: Scientists are not sure what it eats.

Behavior and reproduction: Scientists know little about its behavior outside of the breeding season. During breeding, males call with two short notes. Females answer the calls, and male and female pairs form. The male climbs onto the female's back and grips her by her front legs. She then lays her small eggs. The eggs hatch into long, pointy-snouted, small-mouthed tadpoles. The tadpoles grow in the water until they turn into froglets.

Pointed-tongue floating frogs and people: People rarely see this frog.

Conservation status: The IUCN does not consider this frog to be at risk. It lives over a large area and is usually quite common. ■

Bullfrog (*Rana catesbeiana*)

BULLFROG
Rana catesbeiana

Physical characteristics: The largest frog in North America, the bullfrog can grow to 8 inches (20.3 centimeters) and weigh more than 3.3 pounds (1.5 kilograms). It may be green, brown, or greenish brown, sometimes marked with dark spots on its back and legs. It has long, strong hind legs with toes that have full webs between them. It has a pair of large eardrums showing on each side of the head. Males and females look much alike, except the male's throat is yellowish and the female's is cream-colored, and the male's eardrum is much larger than the eye, while the female's is about the same size as the eye. The bullfrog looks similar to another species, known as the green frog (*Rana clamitans*). The green frog, however, is smaller and has a fold of skin running down each side of the back. The

bullfrog does not have these long folds. Instead, it has a smaller fold that curls from the back of the eye around the eardrum.

Geographic range: The bullfrog is an eastern North American species that lives in northern Mexico, the United States, and southern Canada. Over the years, it has also been introduced to other places in the world, where it does very well including parts of Central and South America, the West Indies, several countries in Europe and southeastern Asia, and some ocean islands, including Hawaii.

Habitat: It makes its home in almost any large, calm body of water, including ponds, bays of the Great Lakes, slow backwaters of rivers and streams, and marshes that are filled with water all year long. Adults are not found in wetlands that dry up for part of the year. In Hawaii, some bullfrogs can even survive in somewhat salty water.

Diet: Bullfrogs hunt by ambush, which means that they sit still and wait for their meals to come to them. Meals may include other frogs, including bullfrog tadpoles and other, younger bullfrogs; various animals, such as snakes, fish, ducklings, and other birds; and many different kinds of invertebrates, like insects, worms, spiders, and snails.

Behavior and reproduction: It usually stays along the edge of its water body, sitting among reeds and other plants that are in the water or just on shore. This frog is active during warm weather. When the cold autumn temperatures arrive, it buries itself in the muck at the bottom of the water and enters hibernation until warm weather returns in the spring. During the breeding season, which runs from spring to mid-summer, each male will defend his piece of shoreline against other male bullfrogs by first making a short warning call, and if that does not work, by pushing the male frog, sometimes even getting into wrestling matches. Males make loud, deep calls, which some people describe as sounding like a slurred "jug-o-rum." A male and female pair may mate at the calling site or move a sort distance away. A female can lay three thousand to twenty thousand eggs, each of which measures only 0.05 to 0.07 inches (1.2 to 1.7 millimeters) across. The eggs hatch within a week into small tadpoles. Unlike the tadpoles of most other species, which turn into froglets within a few months, bullfrog tadpoles may wait from two to four years and grow to 6.7 inches (17 centimeters) long before making the change.

Bullfrogs and people: Many high school students are familiar with this species as the frog they dissect in biology class. It also has other uses. This frog is captured for food, and its legs are served at restaurants across the United States and elsewhere.

Conservation status: This is a very common frog and is not considered to be at risk. Instead, it has become a pest species in many areas of the world where humans have introduced it. This is because the bullfrog not only competes with other species for their food but also eats the other frogs. ▪

Brown frog (*Rana temporaria*)

BROWN FROG
Rana temporaria

Physical characteristics: The brown frog is sometimes called the European common frog or the grass frog. It is typically a tan frog, but some are darker brown, brownish green, gray, or black, and a few are tinted with red or yellow. Warts are scattered on its back, and these usually sit in small, dark brown blotches. The frog also has dark brown bands on its hind legs. Similar bands on its front legs are usually broken and fainter. It has a light-colored thin fold of skin down each side of its back and a dark patch of color behind each eye. Its head narrows toward the front to a somewhat pointy snout. The front feet are unwebbed, but the hind toes have a good deal of webbing between them. The underside of the frog is usually off-white or yellowish white in males and yellowish white to orange in females. During the mating season, the male's throat becomes blue-colored.

Adults grow to 2.4 to 3.7 inches (6.0 to 9.5 centimeters) long from snout to rump.

Geographic range: It lives throughout Europe.

Habitat: Adults mainly live along the forest floor or in grasses for most of the year. In the north where temperatures are cooler, they stay in lowland areas, but they may live high in mountains in the south, as much as 6,562 feet (2,000 meters) above sea level. The tadpoles develop in wetland areas.

Diet: Although this frog is found in much of Europe and is fairly common, scientists still are unsure what it eats.

Behavior and reproduction: In daytime it stays out of sight in damp areas. It becomes more active at night, when it does much of its hunting. It may also become active on rainy days. In northern climates where the weather turns cold in the winter, the brown frog hibernates at the bottom of a pond or under piles of rotting leaves and plants. As soon as the spring sun has melted the snow and ice from the ground and the frogs awaken, the breeding season begins. Males gather at the water and start calling, sometimes wrestling with one another over the females. To mate, a male climbs on the back of a female. The pair may remain together in this piggyback position for a few days. Each female lays one thousand to four thousand small eggs in shallow water. In about two weeks, the eggs hatch into tadpoles, which grow to as much as 1.77 inches (4.5 centimeters) long before they turn into froglets.

Brown frogs and people: They are common in country gardens and other places near humans. Some people in Europe eat these frogs.

Conservation status: Even though this frog is not considered at risk, some populations of it have become small because of over-collecting for various purposes, such as their use as food or their sale in the pet trade. Ecologists are also concerned about the effects of pollution on the frogs and about the draining of their breeding areas. ■

FOR MORE INFORMATION

Books:

Badger, David. *Frogs*. Stillwater, MN: Voyageur Press, 2000.

Halliday, Tim, and Kraig Adler, eds. *The Encyclopedia of Reptiles and Amphibians (Smithsonian Handbooks)*. New York: Facts on File, 1991.

Harding, James H. *Amphibians and Reptiles of the Great Lakes Region*. Ann Arbor, MI: The University of Michigan Press, 1997.

Mattison, Chris. *Frogs and Toads of the World*. New York: Facts on File Publications, 1987.

Miller, Sara Swan. *Frogs and Toads: The Leggy Leapers*. New York: Franklin Watts, 2000.

Showler, Dave. *Frogs and Toads: A Golden Guide*. New York: St. Martin's Press, 2004.

Tyning, Thomas. *A Guide to Amphibians and Reptiles*. Boston, MA: Little, Brown and Company, 1990.

Periodicals:

Turner, Pamela S. "The Extreme Team." *Odyssey* (May 2002): 26.

Chiang, Mona. "Where Have All the Gopher Frogs Gone?" *Science World* (September 22, 2003): 10.

Milius, Susan. "Singing Frog in China Evokes Whales, Primates." *Science News* (September 14, 2002): 173.

Web sites:

"American Bullfrog." *St. Louis Zoo.* http://www.stlzoo.org/animals/abouttheanimals/amphibians/frogsandtoads/americanbullfrog.htm (accessed on April 14, 2005).

"Bullfrogs." *Kildeer Countryside Virtual Wetlands Preserve.* http://www.twingroves.district96.k12.il.us/Wetlands/Frogs/Bullfrog.html (accessed on April 14, 2005).

"Common Frog." *Reptiles and Amphibians of the UK.* http://www.herpetofauna.co.uk/common_frog.htm (accessed on April 14, 2005).

"Green Invaders." *American Museum of Natural History.* http://www.amnh.org/exhibitions/frogs/featured/index.php (accessed on February 1, 2005).

Mercer, Phil. "Australia Hunts Down Toxic Toads." *BBC News, Sydney.* http://news.bbc.co.uk/2/hi/asia-pacific/4242107.stm (accessed on February 6, 2005).

Ramos, M. *"Rana temporaria." Animal Diversity Web.* http://animaldiversity.ummz.umich.edu/site/accounts/information/Rana_temporaria.html (accessed on February 6, 2005).

"What Is the Biggest Frog?" *All About Frogs.* http://allaboutfrogs.org/weird/strange/big.html (accessed on April 14, 2005).

family

C H A P T E R

PHYSICAL CHARACTERISTICS

The squeakers and cricket frogs have smooth skin without the large warts seen in toads and many other types of frogs. A few, like the Ugandan squeaker, have some warts, but the warts are so small that they almost look like grains of sand. Depending on the species, some of the members of this family are reddish, greenish brown, brown, or almost black. Their toes have no webs between them, but the toes in some species end in large pads. Most have thin front and back legs. A few are burrowers, though, and have heavier legs to help them dig. Some of the burrowers also have thick, shovel-like bumps, or tubercles (TOO-ber-kulz), on the heels of their hind feet, which are also used in digging. Many species in this family grow to less than 1 inch (2.5 centimeters) long from the tip of the snout to the end of the rump, but some can grow much bigger. In many species, the adult's size is enough to tell a male from a female. In some, like the crowned forest frog, the male is much larger than the female, but in others, like the common squeaker, the female is bigger than the male.

Squeakers and cricket frogs are usually split into two groups, called subfamilies, although some scientists think the two sub-families are so different that they should instead each have their own family. Others think the squeakers and cricket frogs should not have their own family at all and should instead be combined into the large family of true frogs, known as Ranidae. Many people disagree with this idea because of the breastbone. The breastbone, or sternum, is made of bone in the true frogs, but is different in the squeakers and cricket frogs. The sternum in squeakers and cricket frogs has some flexible material, called cartilage (CAR-tih-lej), in it. In this volume the squeakers and cricket frogs are all listed together in one family, separate from the true frogs. Inside this family are two subfamilies.

The larger of the two subfamilies is called Arthroleptinae and contains about two-thirds of the 77 species in the entire family. This group includes such species as the common squeaker, Tanner's litter frog, the Bush squeaker, and the Ugandan squeaker. Some of the features that most of these frogs share are a thin crease or ridge of skin that runs down the middle of the back and a dark pattern on the back that may be a row of diamonds, an hourglass, or something similar. The back of Tanner's litter frog, for instance, has a row of V-shaped markings. These patterns may be difficult to see on very dark-colored frogs.

The adult males also have a very long third toe on each of their front feet. Toes are counted from the inside to the outside, or from the big toe to the little toe, if compared to humans. This third toe on the West African screeching frog is as long as its thigh. In some species, the toe may be almost half as long as the frog's entire body. Many of the frogs in this subfamily, which as a group are called arthroleptins, have no teeth. Most of these frogs are small, but the female Tanner's litter frog grows to 2.4 inches (6 centimeters) in length, sometimes longer.

The second subfamily is called Astylosterninae and contains species like the crowned forest frog and the hairy frog, among others. Most of the frogs in this group have large bodies. The male crowned forest frog, for instance, grows to 2.7 inches long, and the male hairy frog can reach 5.2 inches in length. In both of these species, the males are bigger than the females. Members of this subfamily also have sharp, curved bones at the ends of their front toes. These bones poke out of the flesh at the tips of the toes, and sometimes look like claws. The front toes are also usually bent. All of these frogs have teeth on the upper jaw.

MY HOME, MY RAINFOREST

Like thousands of other animals, many squeakers and cricket frogs live in only one place in the world: a tiny spot inside a rainforest. Scientists often do not know much about these animals because rainforests are typically so thick with plants that animals—especially small, secretive species like frogs—can easily remain hidden from sight. People, however, are removing more and more of the rainforests to make the land into farms or to use wood from the trees for building. Since some of the rainforest animals live in very small areas, this kind of destruction can wipe out entire species. Conservationists are now trying to save the rainforests and, in doing so, protect the animals that live there.

GEOGRAPHIC RANGE

The squeakers and cricket frogs are found throughout much of central to southern Africa, but not in the southwest portion of the continent. Some live in lowland forests and others in mountains up to 9,800 feet (3,000 meters) above sea level.

HABITAT

Squeakers and cricket frogs live in hot and humid tropical forests, where they spend much of their time under dead and rotting leaves on the forest floor. Sometimes, those in the subfamily Arthroleptinae will also make their homes in fields that have a good cover of leaves on the ground. Frogs in this subfamily live and breed on land. Members of the other subfamily, Astylosterninae, remain on land for most of the year, often in mountain forests. Some, like the Nsoung long-fingered frogs, hide on land under rocks and stones. Member of this subfamily move into fast-flowing streams and rivers to breed, but they usually stay in calm areas and not in the rushing current.

DIET

The smaller frogs in this family eat invertebrates (in-VER-teh-brehts), which are animals without backbones. In particular, they eat tiny insects, spiders, and other arthropods (AR-throe-pawds). Arthropods are invertebrates that have jointed legs. The larger frogs will eat bigger prey, often anything they can find, capture, and stuff into their mouths. Sometimes, this includes other small frogs.

BEHAVIOR AND REPRODUCTION

For many of the squeakers and cricket frogs, time is spent mainly searching along the forest floor, or the shores of streams and rivers, for something to eat. Some, like Tanner's litter frog, hunt by ambush. In this type of hunting, the frog sits very still in one place, waits for an unsuspecting insect or spider to wander past, and quickly grabs and eats it. Other species, including the Ugandan squeaker, take a more active role and slowly move along the ground looking for insects to eat.

Those frogs that live in meadows and in bright, open forests usually stay out of sight during the day and do their hunting at night. Others that live in thick, shady forests may venture out during the daytime, as well as at night. Whether they are active only at night, or during both night and day, squeakers and cricket frogs will seek shelter under leaves if the weather becomes too dry and stay there until it rains again. Some species dig burrows and remain underground instead. This period when the frogs rest and wait for less-dry weather is called estivation (es-tih-VAY-shun).

The frogs mate during the rainy season, when storms soak the land. Squeakers and cricket frogs are named for the sounds of their calls. Some, like the West African screeching frog, have a little flutter in their calls. The West African screeching frog has a high call that lasts less than a second. Many people think this species, and others with calls like it, sounds like crickets. The common squeaker has a short high peep of a call. The calls of the males in each species draw in females of the same species. Those frogs in the subfamily Arthroleptinae mate and lay their eggs in a moist spot on land. The female Tanner's litter frog, for instance, lays about thirty eggs in a small dip in the ground underneath the leaves.

The female Bush squeaker follows the male's long, high "wheep" or "wheepee" call, pairs with him, and lays eleven to eighty eggs under leaves at the base of a bush or other thick, leafy plant. In some species, like the Ugandan squeaker, the female may lay more than one batch of eggs in one breeding period. Since this species only lives for about six months, these two or more sets of eggs are the only young she will have. The female West African screeching frog also lays more than one set of eggs in a breeding season. In each of her two or three clutches, she usually lays ten to thirty eggs. Like the Ugandan squeaker, the West African screeching frog only lives for about six months.

The eggs of most members of this subfamily are each covered in a capsule of gel. The gel provides extra moisture for the baby frog developing inside. While it is growing inside the egg, scientists call the frog an embryo (EHM-bree-oh). They use this same word to describe other types of animals, such as chickens, snakes, and lizards, while they are inside the egg. In squeakers and cricket frogs, the embryo must remain moist. If the egg were to dry out, the embryo would die. These eggs typically have a large yolk, which feeds the growing embryo until the egg hatches.

In some species, an adult stays with the eggs until they hatch. Bush squeakers are one of the species that have this type of care for the eggs. Instead of hatching into tadpoles, the eggs of the frogs in this subfamily hatch right into froglets. The froglets usually look much like the adults. The froglets of the West African screeching frog, for example, have the same dark, hour-glass-shaped pattern on their backs as the adults do. By the time they are three months old, these froglets are old enough to reproduce themselves.

Frogs in the subfamily Astylosterninae do things a bit differently. Instead of mating and laying their eggs on land, they mate and lay their eggs in a fast-flowing stream or river. The males select a spot off to the side where the water is calm, and they mate with females there. The females lay their eggs in the water. In some species, like the hairy frog, the male stays with the sunken eggs until they hatch. The eggs of species in this subfamily hatch into tadpoles, which usually head out of the calm water and into the rushing flow. Some tadpoles, like those of the hairy frog, have large suckers, which the tadpoles use to grab onto rocks and other surfaces, and fight the current. Other tadpoles, like those of the crowned forest frog, have no suckers, but still swim into the fast waters of the stream or river. The tadpoles change into froglets, which then leave the water for a life on land.

SQUEAKERS, CRICKET FROGS, AND PEOPLE

Some people hunt for and eat the larger species of squeakers and cricket frogs. They do not bother the smaller species. Squeakers and cricket frogs are rare in the pet trade.

CONSERVATION STATUS

The World Conservation Union (IUCN) lists two species, the cave squeaker and the Nsoung long-fingered frog, as being Critically Endangered. Critically Endangered species face an extremely high risk of extinction in the wild. Both the cave squeaker and the Nsoung long-fingered frog live in very small areas. In the case of the cave squeaker, all of the individuals appear to live in just one area in the mountains of eastern Zimbabwe. Scientists have only seen this frog once, when it was first discovered in 1962 in a grassy field and nearby caves on the mountain. This spot on the mountain is part of a national park. Nsoung long-fingered frogs are scattered over several spots in western Cameroon, all of which are high on the south side of a mountain. People have begun cutting down the nearby forests to make way for farmland and other uses. If the frog's tiny habitat is also lost, the frog will be in danger of extinction.

The IUCN lists nine other species as Endangered and facing a very high risk of extinction in the wild. All of the nine species are found only in small areas on mountains. One species lives in Guinea, one in Malawi, one in Tanzania, one in Sierre Leone, three in Cameroon and Nigeria, and two in just Cameroon. In many cases, these species are split up into small groups, each of which lives far away from the others. When a species is separated like this, scientists term it fragmented. In other words, the species is divided into small pieces, or fragments. This is usually not healthy for a species, because the males and females have no chance to mate with males and females from other groups. After many generations of breeding within the same group, some of the young may begin to have birth defects that can be fatal. This problem is seen in other types of animals too. Conservationists also are concerned because the endangered frogs all live in habitats that are being threatened by logging, clearing of the land for farming, or other human activities.

The IUCN considers two more species to be Vulnerable and facing a high risk of extinction in the wild; and three to be Near Threatened, which means they are at risk of becoming threatened with extinction in the future. In addition, it names sixteen as Data Deficient, which means that too little information is available to make a judgment about the threat of extinction. Often, this Data Deficient category is used for species that scientists have heard about, but have not yet studied in any detail. In the case of the squeakers and cricket frogs, more than one-fifth of the 77 species in this family fall under the Data Deficient category.

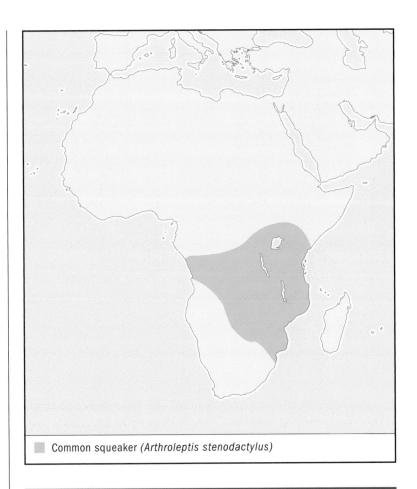

Common squeaker (*Arthroleptis stenodactylus*)

COMMON SQUEAKER
Arthroleptis stenodactylus

Physical characteristics: The common squeaker is sometimes called a dune squeaker or savanna squeaking frog. It is a brown or copper-colored frog with a faded, darker brown pattern on its back that looks something like an hourglass. It has two dark brown spots near the rump and sometimes a thin, lighter-colored stripe running down the middle of the back. It also has dark brown bands on its thin legs. The front legs are quite long compared to the front legs of other frogs, while the rear legs are rather short when compared to many other frogs. It has quite long toes, but no webbing between them. A dark brown line or patch runs from the snout down each side of its face and to its front legs. Its belly is whitish, often with noticeable

but small gray blotches. It has a plump body. Its wide head narrows toward the front, and it has two large, bulging eyes. It is also known as the shovel-footed squeaker because it has a large, rough bump, or tubercle, on each of its back feet. This tubercle, which has a shape something like the edge of a shovel blade, is as long as its first toe. Females and males look much alike, although the male frog has a black throat and a much longer third toe on the front foot. Toes are counted from the inside toe (in humans, the big toe) out. In addition, females are usually larger overall. Females grow to about 1.8 inches (4.5 centimeters) from snout to rump, while males reach about 1.3 inches (3.3 centimeters) when full grown.

Geographic range: The common squeaker lives in much of the southern half of Africa, including parts of the Democratic Republic of the Congo, Kenya, northern South Africa, Zimbabwe, and Mozambique.

Habitat: The common squeaker typically makes its home along the coast in sandy-soiled forests where dead leaves cover the ground. It can live in lowland forests or quite high up on mountainsides. In all, it has been found in places that are from 130 to 6,600 feet (40 to 2,000 meters) above sea level.

Diet: Common squeakers eat many different types of invertebrates, including insects, earthworms, and snails. They may also eat a small frog once in a while.

Behavior and reproduction: When the weather is dry, this frog often stays hidden under damp, dead leaves that lie on the forest floor or beneath grasses in fields. When it rains, however, it will come out during the daytime or at night to look for its next meal. In the breeding season, which is also during the rainy season, the males may use these same hiding places to call day and night for females. The call is a quick, high-pitched peep, similar to the sound a squeaky wheel might make as it spins around. The females lay their eggs in damp places, including little dips in the ground and burrows that are typically under layers of rotting leaves or in tangles of roots at the base of a tree. A female lays about thirty-three to eighty eggs at a time. The eggs are white, about 0.1 inches (2.5 millimeters) in diameter, and are each surrounded in gel. In about one month, these eggs hatch right into froglets, skipping the tadpole stage seen in many other frogs.

Common squeakers and people: The common squeaker does quite well around humans and is often found in gardens. People do not hunt this frog, and it is not common in the pet trade.

Conservation status: The World Conservation Union (IUCN) dos not consider the common squeaker to be at risk. It is very common and found over a large area, including some protected places where logging and other human activities are not allowed. ■

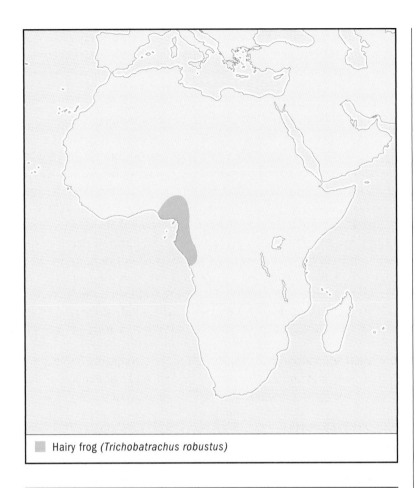

Hairy frog *(Trichobatrachus robustus)*

HAIRY FROG
Trichobatrachus robustus

Physical characteristics: The hairy frog is a large, heavy-bodied frog that is most known for the long frills, or "hairs," that grow only on the males and only during the mating season. These frills are actually very thin bits of flesh that develop on the male's thighs and on the sides of the body from his front legs to the rump. Frogs breathe in oxygen with their lungs and through their skin. Actually, it is the blood vessels in the skin that are able to take up the oxygen. Hairy frogs have very small lungs. Scientists believe that the male's frills help them draw in extra oxygen by giving the frogs more skin, and therefore more blood vessels, through which to breathe. This is important for the

males, which need all the oxygen they can get once they mate and start caring for their young.

Males also have many rough pads on the bottoms of their unwebbed front feet. Their back feet, which are webbed, also have a few pads, but not as many as the front feet have. The pads probably help them hang onto the female during mating. They have very long toes on their back feet. Both males and females are dark greenish brown to black and have a long dark blotch down the center of the back and smaller dark spots toward the rump. In especially dark frogs, the blotch and spots may be difficult to see. Hairy frogs have a yellow throat. Males grow larger than females. Males can reach 5.2 inches (13 centimeters) long, while females reach 3.6 inches (9 centimeters) in length.

Geographic range: Hairy frogs live in the western part of central Africa, including eastern Nigeria, Cameroon, Equatorial Guinea, and parts of the Democratic Republic of the Congo and Gabon. Scientists think it may also live in Angola, although they have not seen any there yet.

Habitat: Hairy frogs especially like to make their homes in areas where thick, lush forests surround fast-flowing streams and rivers. Sometimes, the frogs live on farms, such as tea plantations, but they usually prefer mountain forests. Hairy frogs stay on land nearly all year, but enter the streams and rivers to mate.

Diet: Hairy frogs eat insects and other arthropods that they find along the ground of the forest and the shores of streams.

Behavior and reproduction: Hairy frogs spend most of the year hopping along the forest floor looking for things to eat. When the rainy season comes, their attention turns to mating. Males enter streams and sometimes rivers that have a fast current, but they stay in a quiet spot where the water is very still. After spending a few extra days in the forest, the females join the males in the streams and rivers and mate with them. During mating, the male climbs onto the female's back and holds on near her front legs while she lays her eggs. The pads on his front feet probably help him cling to her body, which is wet and quite slippery.

Each female lays her eggs in the water, and the male stays with them. Water contains oxygen, and the frog's skin, including the frills on his sides and legs, take up this oxygen so the frog can breathe even when he is completely underwater. For this reason, the male can stay beneath the surface with the eggs for days without having to come up for air. The eggs hatch into tadpoles that have a large sucker on the belly side. The sucker helps them attach to rocks and other surfaces in the water. The tadpoles continue to live there, sometimes even venturing into the tumbling foam at the bottom of small waterfalls, before turning into froglets and climbing out onto land.

Hairy frogs and people: Some people collect and eat these large frogs and even the tadpoles. In places where a great deal of hunting takes place, the frogs can become scarce.

Conservation status: Although people do hunt the frogs for their meat, the World COnservation Union (IUCN) does not consider the species to be at risk for now, because the frogs live over a fairly large area, are quite common, and are not hunted everywhere they live. Conservationists are, however, keeping a watchful eye on the frogs. Some streams and rivers where the frogs mate are becoming more polluted, and this may be killing a number of the eggs, tadpoles, and/or frogs. ∎

FOR MORE INFORMATION

Books:

Channing, Alan. *Amphibians of Central and Southern Africa.* Ithaca, NY: Comstock Publishing Associates, 2001.

Passmore, Neville, and Vincent Carruthers. *South African Frogs: A Complete Guide.* Revised edition. Halfway House, South Africa: Southern Book Publishers and Johannesburg: Witwatersrand University Press, 1995.

Rödel, Mark-Oliver. *Herpetofauna of West Africa.* Vol. 1, *Amphibians of the West African Savanna.* Frankfurt: Chimaira, 2000.

Showler, Dave. *Frogs and Toads: A Golden Guide.* New York: St. Martin's Press, 2004.

Web sites:

"Breathing." *The Frog.* http://www.thefrog.org/biology/breathing/breathing.htm (accessed on April 10, 2005).

"Common Squeaker." *Herpetology Department, California Academy of Sciences.* http://www.calacademy.org/research/herpetology/frogs/list6.html (accessed on April 10, 2005).

"South Malawi Montane Forest-Grassland Mosaic." *World Wildlife Fund.* http://www.worldwildlife.org/wildworld/profiles/terrestrial/at/at014_full.html (accessed on April 10, 2005).

Class: Amphibia

Order: Anura

Family: Hemisotidae

Number of species: About 9 or 10 species

family

CHAPTER

PHYSICAL CHARACTERISTICS

The species of shovel-nosed frogs have wide, rounded, and rather flattened bodies with thick, strong front and rear legs. The very short front toes have no webs between them. The hind toes, which are much longer than the front toes, have a little webbing in some species, but no webbing in others. The spotted snout-burrower, for instance, has no webbing between its back toes. The head of all species is short and blends back into the body without a noticeable neck. The frogs have rather small eyes with vertical pupils and a pointed snout with a hard, sharp end. This makes the snout look a bit like the edge of a shovel blade. The tongue in these frogs has a notch in the tip. They also have a groove or fold that runs across the top of the head from behind one eye to behind the other.

A close look at the heels of the rear feet reveals a large, flat bump, or tubercle (TOO-ber-kul). The tubercle, which is hard and rough like the callous a person might get on his or her hand, is located on the inside of each heel.

Beneath the skin, the shovel-nosed frogs have a thick skeleton, which gives them a very solid body. The bones in much of the frogs' front and back feet, not including the toe bones, are fused together for added strength. The shovel-nosed frogs do not, however, have a breastbone, also known as the sternum.

Many frogs in this family are brown or purple with yellow markings. The spotted snout-burrower, for example, is dark purple or brown with small yellow spots. The marbled snout-burrower is a bit different. It may have a brown or a dark green head and back. The back is covered with numerous dark brown to black blotches. Its head often has noticeable dark stripes extending from the snout past the eye and to the back of the head. Its sides and legs have yellow- to cream-colored speckles.

Many of the shovel-nosed frogs are quite small and only reach 1 inch (2.5 centimeters) long from snout to rump. The spotted snout-burrower is an exception. This species, the biggest member of the family, grows to 3 inches (8 centimeters) long.

GEOGRAPHIC RANGE

Shovel-nosed frogs live in central and southern Africa, a region known as Sub-Saharan Africa. In particular, the frogs make their homes in a stretch of land from the west coast of central Africa across to Ethiopia in the east, down the east coast, and back across to the west side of the continent around Angola. Some, like the marbled snout-burrower and Guinea snout-burrower, live over a very large area, including many countries in Africa. Others live in very small areas. In 2002, a new species was found in western Zambia, which is in southern Africa, but nowhere else. The Ethiopian snout-burrower, which is also known as the Lake Zwai snout-burrower, is only known to live in parts of Ethiopia.

HABITAT

Shovel-nosed frogs live underground in dry, grassy areas. During the wet season, however, the rains fill the land with small, deep pools of water, and the frogs come out to feed and to mate. They lay their eggs underground, but the tadpoles move into these pools of water or in other small ponds that remain filled with water all year and develop there. Shovel-nosed frogs may live in lowland areas or in places as high as 5,900 feet (1,800 meters) above sea level.

DIET

These frogs search for food during the rainy season. At night, they may look about on land for insects. They are also good diggers and put this talent to use when finding a meal. They tunnel along just a few inches below the surface and seek out termites and earthworms there.

BEHAVIOR AND REPRODUCTION

The strong body, muscular legs, heavy skeleton, and shovel-like snout together help these frogs to be excellent diggers. They all dig head first into the muddy banks near water pools or small ponds, moving the head up and down to take advantage of the "shovel nose" to push away soil. Even the tubercles on the heels of their hind feet give them an added push when they are forcing their front ends into the ground. Most other burrowing frogs use their rear legs as the main digging limbs and dig themselves backward into the soil. During the dry season of the year, the frogs stay in their burrows and rest. This resting period during dry weather is called estivation (es-tih-VAY-shun). When the rains come, the frogs come out to look for food or to mate.

When the mating season starts, the males call to attract females. They call from the ground in a hiding spot under plants next to a pool of water or small pond. The call is a long buzzing sound. The call of a male marbled snout-burrower, for instance, is a buzz that lasts about two seconds. When a female pairs up with a male, he crawls onto her back and holds on as she starts digging head first into the ground to make a burrow under a log or stone. With the male still on her back, she continues tunneling. When the pair are completely buried, she lays a clump of one hundred fifty to two hundred eggs, although some females only lay about three dozen eggs. Each egg is about 0.1 inches (2 to 2.5 millimeters) in diameter and has a capsule around it.

A PINCH OF THIS, A DASH OF THAT

Depending on which features a scientist considers, the shovel-nosed frogs may look a bit like frogs in other families. As a result, researchers have had a hard time figuring out where the shovel-nosed frogs belong. Some think they should really be listed as part of another family. These families include the true frogs in the family Ranidae, which share several characteristics with the shovel-nosed frogs including a notched tongue tip; the rain frogs, which are members of the family Microhylidae and are burrowers like the shovel-nosed frogs are; and the African treefrogs of the family Hyperoliidae, which have vertical pupils in their eyes like those in the shovel-nosed frogs. Other scientists, however, consider the shovel-nosed frogs to be unusual enough to be listed in their own family, as they are in this volume.

After mating, the male digs back out of the ground and leaves, but the female stays behind with her eggs. As the eggs develop, rains continue to fall, eventually filling the pools and ponds. Water overflows and soon rises to cover and soak into the underground chamber where the female is staying with her eggs. By this time, usually less than two weeks later, the eggs begin to hatch into tadpoles. The female may dig a tunnel out of the burrow. The tadpoles use the tunnel to swim in the flooding water, out of the chamber, and into the pools and ponds. If the tadpoles hatch before the nest chamber is flooded, or in a year when the rains are not hard enough to overflow the pool or pond and flood the nest, the tadpoles in some species scramble onto the female's back, and she carries them out of the nest and to the water.

SHOVEL-NOSED FROGS AND PEOPLE

People rarely see this frog, which remains underground much of the year.

CONSERVATION STATUS

Of the nine or ten species in this family, the World Conservation Union (IUCN) considers one to be Vulnerable and facing a high risk of extinction in the wild; and four to be Data Deficient, which means that too little information is available to make a judgment about the threat of extinction. The Vulnerable species is the spotted snout-burrower, which is found in South Africa and probably in Swaziland, although scientists have not yet discovered it there. Members of this species live in groups, or populations, in several small areas that are separated from one another. The future of the frogs is threatened by the clearing of trees and plants in the frog's habitat. People clear the land to make way for sugar cane farms and housing developments. Fortunately, some of the frogs live in several protected areas, including parks, where land cannot be cleared. People are also, however, introducing fishes to the pools of water and small ponds that the frogs use for breeding. Often, these fishes eat the frogs and/or their tadpoles.

The four species listed as Data Deficient include the Masiliwa snout-burrower, Perret's snout-burrower, De Witte's snout-burrower, and a species known only by its scientific name of *Hemisus barotseensis*. Scientists have not done thorough searches for the Masiliwa snout-burrower or for De Witte's snout-burrower for many years and know little about either species. Perret's snout-burrower, which is found in Congo and Gabon, is rarely seen. Since it usually stays underground, however, it may be more common than it appears. Scientists also know little about *Hemisus barotseensis*, which was just discovered in 2002.

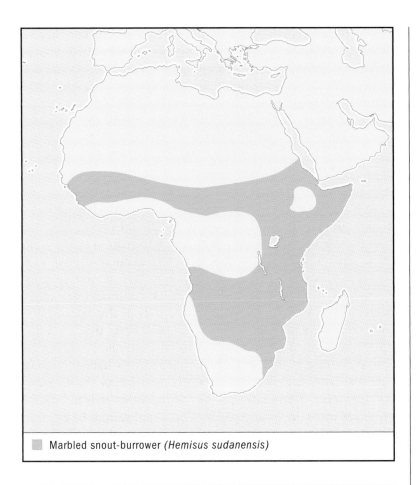

Marbled snout-burrower *(Hemisus sudanensis)*

MARBLED SNOUT-BURROWER
Hemisus sudanensis

Physical characteristics: The marbled snout-burrower also goes by the common names of marbled shovel-nosed frog, mottled shovel-nosed frog, pig-nosed frog, and mottled burrowing frog. The marbled snout-burrower is typically brown with darker brown markings on its back and head and often a light-colored stripe down the middle of the back. Its back toes have a little webbing, but the front toes have none. Its front legs are thick and strong. Females sometimes grow to as much as 2.2 inches (5.5 centimeters) long from snout to rump. Some scientists consider this frog not to be a separate species, but instead to be a subspecies of another species, known as *Hemisus marmatorus*. Sometimes species are split into one or more subspecies.

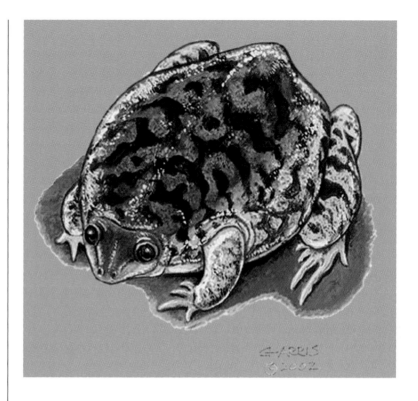

This means that the frogs are still members of the same species, but are slightly different. Perhaps they live in separate places or have slightly unusual looks or behaviors.

Geographic range: It lives in much of central and southern Africa.

Habitat: This is a burrowing frog that spends most of the year underground in dry areas, often with few if any trees.

Diet: Marbled snout-burrowers eat a variety of insects above and below the ground.

Behavior and reproduction: Much of the time, marbled snout-burrowers search for and eat various insects that they either find along the ground or in the underground tunnels that they dig. They are especially fond of termites, particularly when the termites develop wings, which they do during part of their life cycle, and leave their termite hills. The frogs wait near the exits to the hills and grab the termites as they fly out.

The frogs mate and have their young next to pools of water or small ponds that remain filled with water all year. Males call and attract females. When a female approaches a male, he grabs hold of her, and she begins digging head first into the soft mud near but outside the pool or pond. When she has dug out a burrow—with the male still clinging to her—she lays her eggs inside the underground nest chamber. The male leaves, but the female stays with her eggs as they hatch into tadpoles underground. When rains come, the pool or pond overflows and soaks the burrow. The tadpoles then swim out. If too little rain falls and the burrow does not flood, scientists think that the tadpoles probably squirm onto the female's back and she carries them out of the burrow and into the nearby pool or pond. In that water body, the tadpoles develop into froglets.

Marbled snout-burrowers and people: People rarely see this mainly underground frog.

Conservation status: The World Conservation Union (IUCN) lists only nine species of shovel-nosed frogs and does not consider this species to be separate from *Hemisus marmatorus*. According to the IUCN, *Hemisus marmatorus* is not at particular risk. It lives over a large part of Africa, including protected areas, and is probably quite common.   ■

FOR MORE INFORMATION

Books:

Burnie, David, and Don E. Wilson. *Animal.* New York: DK Publishing Inc., 2001.

Channing, A. *Amphibians of Central and Southern Africa.* Ithaca, NY: Cornell University Press, 2001.

Showler, Dave. *Frogs and Toads: A Golden Guide.* New York: St. Martin's Press, 2004.

Web sites:

Cannatella, David. *"Hemisus." Tree of Life Web Project.* http://tolweb.org/tree?group=Hemisus&contgroup=Neobatrachia (accessed on February 21, 2005).

"Hemisus marmoratum." Amphibans (Mamoru Kawamura). http://www.rieo.net/amph/exfrog/aka/hemisus/marmo.htm (accessed on February 21, 2005).

"Hemisus marmoratum." California Academy of Sciences. http://www.calacademy.org/research/herpetology/frogs/list7.html (accessed on February 21, 2005).

Species List by Biome

CONIFEROUS FOREST

Ailao moustache toad
Annam broad-headed toad
Bana leaf litter frog
Brown frog
Cascade torrent salamander
Coastal giant salamander
Eastern narrow-mouthed toad
European fire salamander
Fire-bellied toad
Great crested newt
Mandarin salamander
Oriental fire-bellied toad
Schmidt's lazy toad
Smooth newt
Two-lined salamander
Yellow-bellied toad

DECIDUOUS FOREST

Arboreal salamander
Asian horned frog
Bell's salamander
Brown frog
Cascade torrent salamander
Common squeaker
Darwin's frog
Eastern narrow-mouthed toad
European fire salamander
Fire-bellied toad

Golden-striped salamander
Goliath frog
Great crested newt
Green treefrog
Hairy frog
Hamilton's frog
Harlequin frog
Kinugasa flying frog
Lynch's Cochran frog
Mandarin salamander
Marine toad
Maud Island frog
Mesoamerican burrowing toad
Mexican caecilian
Micro frog
Mocquard's rain frog
Natal ghost frog
Nilgiri tropical frog
Oriental fire-bellied toad
Pacific giant glass frog
Painted frog
Painted Indonesian treefrog
Painted reed frog
Paradox frog
Parsley frog
Phantasmal poison frog
Pumpkin toadlet
Rock River frog
Rocky Mountain tailed frog
Ruthven's frog

South American bullfrog
Smooth newt
Sumaco horned treefrog
Talamancan web-footed
   salamander
Tusked frog
Two-lined salamander
Yellow-bellied toad
Yucatecan shovel-headed
   treefrog

DESERT

Sandhill frog
Water-holding frog

GRASSLAND

Asian horned frog
Banded rubber frog
Brown frog
Bubbling kassina
Budgett's frog
Darwin's frog
Fire-bellied toad
Gray four-eyed frog
Great crested newt
Mandarin salamander
Marbled snout-burrower
Marine toad
Mesoamerican burrowing toad

Mocquard's rain frog
Natal ghost frog
Northern spadefoot toad
Oriental fire-bellied toad
Painted frog
Painted reed frog
Paradox frog
Parsley frog
Patagonia frog
Plains spadefoot toad
Pointed-tongue floating frog
Riobamba marsupial frog
Smooth newt
Tiger salamander
Tusked frog
Yellow-bellied toad
Yucatecan shovel-headed
  treefrog
Water-holding frog

LAKE AND POND
Amazonian skittering frog
Brown frog
Bubbling kassina
Bullfrog
Common plantanna (African
  clawed frog)
Eastern narrow-mouthed toad
Fire-bellied toad
Golden-striped salamander
Gray four-eyed frog
Great crested newt
Hokkaido salamander
Hourglass treefrog
Japanese fire-bellied newt
Lesser siren
Mandarin salamander
Marine toad
Midwife toad
Mudpuppy
Olm
Oriental fire-bellied toad
Painted frog
Painted reed frog
Paradox frog
Patagonia frog

Perez's snouted frog
Phantasmal poison frog
Philippine barbourula
Pointed-tongue floating frog
Pyburn's pancake frog
Riobamba marsupial frog
Smooth newt
South American bullfrog
Surinam horned frog
Surinam toad
Three-toed amphiuma
Tropical clawed frog
Two-lined salamander
Yellow-bellied toad

RAINFOREST
African wart frog
Amazonian skittering frog
Blue-toed rocket frog
Eungella torrent frog
Free Madagascar frog
Golden dart-poison frog
Golden toad
Gold-striped frog
Hip pocket frog
Hourglass treefrog
Kirk's caecilian
La Palma glass frog
Long-fingered slender toad
Marbled caecilian
Perez's snouted frog
Philippine barbourula
Pyburn's pancake frog
Red caecilian
Ruthven's frog
Seychelles frog
South American bullfrog
Surinam horned frog
Tusked frog
Wilhelm rainforest frog

RIVER AND STREAM
Ailao moustache toad
Annam broad-headed toad
Asian horned frog

Brown frog
Bullfrog
Cascade torrent salamander
Cayenne caecilian
Ceylon caecilian
Coastal giant salamander
Common plantanna (African
  clawed frog)
Darwin's frog
Dusky salamander
Eungella torrent frog
Fire-bellied toad
Goliath frog
Green treefrog
Hairy frog
Harlequin frog
Hellbender
Hokkaido salamander
Japanese clawed salamander
La Palma glass frog
Lesser siren
Long-fingered slender toad
Lynch's Cochran frog
Marbled caecilian
Midwife toad
Mudpuppy
Natal ghost frog
Nilgiri tropical frog
Olm
Oriental fire-bellied toad
Painted frog
Painted reed frog
Paradox frog
Phantasmal poison frog
Philippine barbourula
Pyburn's pancake frog
Rock River frog
Rocky Mountain tailed frog
Ruthven's frog
Schmidt's lazy toad
Semirechensk salamander
South American bullfrog
Surinam toad
Texas blind salamander
Three-toed amphiuma

Tropical clawed frog
Two-lined salamander
Yellow-bellied toad

WETLAND
Banded rubber frog
Bubbling kassina
Budgett's frog
Brown frog
Bullfrog
Ceylon caecilian
Common plantanna (African
  clawed frog)
Darwin's frog

Eastern narrow-mouthed toad
Fire-bellied toad
Free Madagascar frog
Green treefrog
Kinugasa flying frog
Kirk's caecilian
Lesser siren
Malaysian painted frog
Marbled snout-burrower
Marine toad
Micro frog
Mocquard's rain frog
Northern spadefoot toad
Oriental fire-bellied toad
Painted frog

Painted reed frog
Paradox frog
Perez's snouted frog
Pointed-tongue floating frog
Riobamba marsupial frog
Ruthven's frog
Schmidt's lazy toad
Semirechensk salamander
Surinam horned frog
Surinam toad
Three-toed amphiuma
Yellow-bellied toad
Yucatecan shovel-headed
  treefrog
Water-holding frog

Species List by Geographic Range

ALBANIA
Brown frog
European fire salamander
Great crested newt
Smooth newt

ALGERIA
Painted frog

ANDORRA
European fire salamander
Great crested newt
Smooth newt

ANGOLA
Bubbling kassina
Common plantanna (African
  clawed frog)
Hairy frog
Marbled snout-burrower
Painted reed frog
Tropical clawed frog

ARGENTINA
Budgett's frog
Darwin's frog
Gray four-eyed frog
Marine toad

Patagonia frog

ARMENIA
Brown frog

AUSTRALIA
Eungella torrent frog
Green treefrog
Hip pocket frog
Marine toad
Northern spadefoot toad
Painted frog
Sandhill frog
Tusked frog
Water-holding frog

AUSTRIA
Brown frog
European fire salamander
Fire-bellied toad
Great crested newt
Smooth newt
Yellow-bellied toad

BAHAMAS
Eastern narrow-mouthed toad

BELARUS
European fire salamander
Great crested newt
Smooth newt

BELGIUM
Brown frog
European fire salamander
Great crested newt
Midwife toad
Parsley frog
Smooth newt

BELIZE
Marine toad
Mesoamerican burrowing toad
Mexican caecilian
Yucatecan shovel-headed
  treefrog

BENIN
Bubbling Kassina
Goliath frog
Painted reed frog

BOLIVIA
Amazonian skittering frog
Budgett's frog

Hourglass treefrog
Marine toad
Perez's snouted frog
Surinam toad

BOSNIA AND HERZEGOVINA
European fire salamander
Great crested newt
Olm
Smooth newt

BOTSWANA
Bubbling kassina
Common plantanna (African clawed frog)
Painted reed frog

BRAZIL
Amazonian skittering frog
Blue-toed rocket frog
Cayenne caecilian
Gold-striped frog
Hourglass treefrog
Marine toad
Paradox frog
Perez's snouted frog
Pumpkin toadlet
Rock River frog
Ruthven's frog
South American bullfrog
Surinam horned frog
Surinam toad

BULGARIA
European fire salamander
Great crested newt
Smooth newt

BURKINA FASO
Bubbling kassina
Painted reed frog

BURUNDI
Bubbling kassina
Common plantanna (African clawed frog)
Painted reed frog

CAMBODIA
Pointed-tongue floating frog

CAMEROON
African wart frog
Bubbling kassina
Common plantanna (African clawed frog)
Goliath frog
Hairy frog
Marbled snout-burrower
Painted reed frog
Tropical clawed frog

CANADA
Bullfrog
Coastal giant salamander
Coastal tailed frog
Dusky salamander
Mudpuppy
Plains spadefoot toad
Rocky Mountain tailed frog
Tiger salamander
Two-lined salamander

CHAD
Bubbling kassina
Painted reed frog

CHILE
Common plantanna (African clawed frog)
Darwin's frog
Gray four-eyed frog
Marine toad

CHINA
Ailao moustache toad

Malaysian painted frog
Mandarin salamander
Oriental fire-bellied toad
Pointed-tongue floating frog
Schmidt's lazy toad
Semirechensk salamander

COLOMBIA
Amazonian skittering frog
Cayenne caecilian
Golden dart-poison frog
Gold-striped frog
Hourglass treefrog
La Palma glass frog
Lynch's Cochran frog
Marine toad
Pacific giant glass frog
Perez's snouted frog
Pyburn's pancake frog
South American bullfrog
Sumaco horned treefrog
Surinam horned frog
Surinam toad

COSTA RICA
Golden toad
Harlequin frog
La Palma glass frog
Marine toad
Mesoamerican burrowing toad
Mexican caecilian
South American bullfrog
Talamancan web-footed salamander

CROATIA
European fire salamander
Great crested newt
Olm
Smooth newt

CYPRUS
Brown frog

CZECH REPUBLIC
Brown frog
European fire salamander
Great crested newt
Smooth newt

DEMOCRATIC REPUBLIC OF THE CONGO
Common plantanna (African clawed frog)
Common squeaker
Hairy frog
Marbled snout-burrower

DENMARK
Brown frog
European fire salamander
Fire-bellied toad
Great crested newt
Smooth newt

ECUADOR
Hourglass treefrog
La Palma glass frog
Marbled caecilian
Marine toad
Pacific giant glass frog
Phantasmal poison frog
Riobamba marsupial frog
South American bullfrog
Sumaco horned treefrog
Surinam toad

EL SALVADOR
Marine toad
Mesoamerican burrowing toad
Mexican caecilian

EQUATORIAL GUINEA
Common plantanna (African clawed frog)
Hairy frog

Marbled snout-burrower

ESTONIA
Brown frog
European fire salamander
Great crested newt
Smooth newt

ETHIOPIA
Bubbling kassina
Ethiopian snout-burrower (Lake Zwai snout-burrower)
Painted reed frog

FINLAND
Brown frog
European fire salamander
Great crested newt
Smooth newt

FRANCE
Brown frog
European fire salamander
Great crested newt
Midwife toad
Painted frog
Parsley frog
Smooth newt

FRENCH GUIANA
Cayenne caecilian
Gold-striped frog
Hourglass treefrog
Marine toad
Paradox frog
Pyburn's pancake frog
Ruthven's frog
South American bullfrog
Surinam toad
Surinam horned frog

GABON
African wart frog

Bubbling kassina
Common plantanna (African clawed frog)
Hairy frog
Marbled snout-burrower
Painted reed frog
Tropical clawed frog

GERMANY
Brown frog
Common plantanna (African clawed frog)
European fire salamander
Fire-bellied toad
Great crested newt
Midwife toad
Smooth newt

GHANA
Bubbling kassina
Goliath frog
Painted reed frog

GREECE
Brown frog
European fire salamander
Fire-bellied toad
Great crested newt
Smooth newt
Yellow-bellied toad

GUATEMALA
Marine toad
Mesoamerican burrowing toad
Mexican caecilian
Yucatecan shovel-headed treefrog

GUINEA
Bubbling kassina
Goliath frog
Painted reed frog

GUINEA-BISSAU
Bubbling kassina
Painted reed frog

GUYANA
Cayenne caecilian
Gold-striped frog
Hourglass treefrog
Marine toad
Paradox frog
Pyburn's pancake frog
Ruthven's frog
South American bullfrog
Surinam horned frog
Surinam toad

HONDURAS
Marine toad
Mesoamerican burrowing toad
Mexican caecilian
South American bullfrog
Yucatecan shovel-headed
  treefrog

HUNGARY
Brown frog
European fire salamander
Great crested newt
Smooth newt
Yellow-bellied toad

INDIA
Mandarin salamander
Nilgiri tropical frog
Pointed-tongue floating frog
Red caecilian

INDONESIA
Asian horned frog
Long-fingered slender toad
Malaysian painted frog
Painted Indonesian treefrog
Pointed-tongue floating frog

IRELAND
European fire salamander
Great crested newt
Smooth newt

ITALY
Brown frog
European fire salamander
Great crested newt
Olm
Painted frog
Parsley frog
Smooth newt
Yellow-bellied toad

IVORY COAST
Bubbling kassina
Goliath frog
Painted reed frog

JAPAN
Hokkaido salamander
Japanese clawed salamander
Japanese fire-bellied newt
Kinugasa flying frog
Marine toad
Oriental fire-bellied toad

KAZAKHSTAN
Semirechensk salamander

KENYA
Banded rubber frog
Bubbling kassina
Common plantanna (African
  clawed frog)
Common squeaker
Marbled snout-burrower
Painted reed frog

KOREA
(NORTH AND SOUTH)
Oriental fire-bellied toad

LAOS
Bana leaf litter frog

LATVIA
European fire salamander
Great crested newt
Smooth newt

LESOTHO
Bubbling kassina
Common plantanna (African
  clawed frog)
Natal ghost frog
Painted reed frog
Tropical clawed frog

LIBERIA
Bubbling kassina
Goliath frog
Painted reed frog

LIECHTENSTEIN
European fire salamander
Great crested newt
Smooth newt

LITHUANIA
European fire salamander
Great crested newt
Smooth newt

LUXEMBOURG
Brown frog
European fire salamander
Great crested newt
Midwife toad
Parsley frog
Smooth newt

MACEDONIA
European fire salamander
Great crested newt
Smooth newt

MADAGASCAR
Free Madagascar frog
Mocquard's rain frog

MALAWI
Bubbling kassina
Common plantanna (African
  clawed frog)
Kirk's caecilian
Painted reed frog

MALAYSIA
Asian horned frog
Malaysian painted frog
Painted Indonesian treefrog
Pointed-tongue floating frog

MALI
Bubbling kassina
Painted reed frog

MALTA
Brown frog
European fire salamander
Great crested newt
Painted frog
Smooth newt

MEXICO
Arboreal salamander
Bell's salamander
Bullfrog
Lesser siren
Marine toad
Mesoamerican burrowing toad
Mexican caecilian
Plains spadefoot toad
Tiger salamander
Yucatecan shovel-headed
  treefrog

MOLDOVA
European fire salamander

Great crested newt
Smooth newt

MONACO
European fire salamander
Great crested newt
Smooth newt

MOROCCO
Painted frog

MOZAMBIQUE
Banded rubber frog
Bubbling kassina
Common plantanna (African
  clawed frog)
Common squeaker
Marbled snout-burrower
Painted reed frog

NAMIBIA
Bubbling kassina
Common plantanna (African
  clawed frog)
Painted reed frog
Tropical clawed frog

NEPAL
Mandarin salamander

NETHERLANDS
Brown frog
European fire salamander
Great crested newt
Midwife toad
Smooth newt

NEW ZEALAND
Green treefrog
Hamilton's frog
Maud Island frog

NICARAGUA
Marine toad
Mesoamerican burrowing toad
Mexican caecilian
South American bullfrog

NIGER
Bubbling kassina
Painted reed frog

NIGERIA
Bubbling kassina
Goliath frog
Hairy frog
Marbled snout-burrower
Painted reed frog

NORWAY
Brown frog
European fire salamander
Great crested newt
Smooth newt

PANAMA
Harlequin frog
La Palma glass frog
Marine toad
Mexican caecilian
South American bullfrog

PAPUA NEW GUINEA
Wilhelm rainforest frog

PARAGUAY
Budgett's frog
Marine toad

PERU
Amazonian skittering frog
Cayenne caecilian
Gold-striped frog
Hourglass treefrog

Marine toad
Perez's snouted frog
Phantasmal poison frog
Ruthven's frog
South American bullfrog
Sumaco horned treefrog
Surinam toad
Surinam horned frog

PHILIPPINES
Asian horned frog
Marine toad
Painted Indonesian treefrog
Philippine barbourula

POLAND
European fire salamander
Fire-bellied toad
Great crested newt
Smooth newt

PORTUGAL
Brown frog
European fire salamander
Golden-striped salamander
Great crested newt
Midwife toad
Parsley frog
Smooth newt

REPUBLIC OF THE CONGO
African wart frog
Common plantanna (African clawed frog)
Tropical clawed frog

ROMANIA
European fire salamander
Great crested newt
Smooth newt

RUSSIA

European fire salamander
Great crested newt
Oriental fire-bellied toad
Smooth newt

RWANDA
Bubbling kassina
Common plantanna (African clawed frog)
Painted reed frog

SAN MARINO
European fire salamander
Great crested newt
Smooth newt

SÃO TOMÉ AND PRÍNCIPE
Common plantanna (African clawed frog)

SENEGAL
Bubbling kassina
Painted reed frog

SERBIA-MONTENEGRO
European fire salamander
Great crested newt
Olm
Smooth newt

SEYCHELLES
Seychelles frog

SIERRA LEONE
Bubbling kassina
Goliath frog
Painted reed frog

SINGAPORE
Painted Indonesian treefrog

SLOVAKIA
European fire salamander
Great crested newt
Smooth newt

SLOVENIA
European fire salamander
Great crested newt
Olm
Smooth newt

SOMALIA
Banded rubber frog

SOUTH AFRICA
Banded rubber frog
Bubbling kassina
Common plantanna (African clawed frog)
Common squeaker
Marbled snout-burrower
Micro frog
Natal ghost frog
Painted reed frog
Tropical clawed frog

SPAIN
Brown frog
European fire salamander
Golden-striped salamander
Great crested newt
Midwife toad
Painted frog
Parsley frog
Smooth newt

SRI LANKA
Ceylon caecilian

SUDAN
Bubbling kassina
Painted reed frog

SURINAME
Cayenne caecilian
Gold-striped frog
Hourglass treefrog
Marine toad
Paradox frog
Pyburn's pancake frog
Ruthven's frog
South American bullfrog
Surinam horned frog
Surinam toad

SWAZILAND
Bubbling kassina
Common plantanna (African
  clawed frog)
Natal ghost frog
Painted reed frog

SWEDEN
Brown frog
European fire salamander
Fire-bellied toad
Great crested newt
Smooth newt

SWITZERLAND
Brown frog
European fire salamander
Great crested newt
Midwife toad
Smooth newt
Yellow-bellied toad

TAIWAN
Malaysian painted frog
Painted Indonesian treefrog

TANZANIA
Banded rubber frog
Bubbling kassina
Common plantanna (African
  clawed frog)
Kirk's caecilian

Painted reed frog

THAILAND
Asian horned frog
Mandarin salamander

TOGO
Bubbling kassina
Goliath frog
Painted reed frog

TRINIDAD AND TOBAGO
Surinam toad

TUNISIA
Painted frog

TURKEY
Brown frog
European fire salamander
Fire-bellied toad
Great crested newt
Smooth newt

UGANDA
Bubbling kassina
Common plantanna (African
  clawed frog)
Painted reed frog

UKRAINE
European fire salamander
Great crested newt
Smooth newt

UNITED KINGDOM
Common plantanna (African
  clawed frog)
European fire salamander
Fire-bellied toad
Great crested newt
Smooth newt

Yellow-bellied toad

UNITED STATES
Arboreal salamander
Bullfrog
Cascade torrent salamander
Coastal giant salamander
Coastal tailed frog
Common plantanna (African
  clawed frog)
Dusky salamander
Eastern narrow-mouthed toad
Hellbender
Lesser siren
Marine toad
Mesoamerican burrowing toad
Mudpuppy
Plains spadefoot toad
Rocky Mountain tailed frog
Texas blind salamander
Three-toed amphiuma
Tiger salamander
Two-lined salamander

URUGUAY
Marine toad
Paradox frog

VENEZUELA
Marine toad
Paradox frog
Pyburn's pancake frog
Ruthven's frog
Surinam toad

VIETNAM
Ailao moustache toad
Annam broad-headed toad
Bana leaf litter frog
Mandarin salamander
Pointed-tongue floating frog

ZAMBIA
Bubbling kassina

Common plantanna (African
  clawed frog)
Painted reed frog

Bubbling kassina
Common plantanna (African
  clawed frog)

Common squeaker
Marbled snout-burrower
Painted reed frog

Index

Italic type indicates volume number; **boldface** type indicates entries and their pages; (ill.) indicates illustrations.

Asian tailed caecilians, *3:* 511–16

Asian toadfrogs, *1:* 77–93

Asian treefrogs, *3:*350–67

Asiatic giant salamanders, *3:* 419–26

Asiatic salamanders, *3:* 409–18

Assa darlingtoni. See Hip pocket frogs

Astylosterninae, *2:* 311, 314

Atelognathus patagonicus. See Patagonia frogs

Atelopus varius. See Harlequin frogs

Atelopus vogli, 2: 203

Athroleptinae, *2:* 312

Atrato glass frogs, *2:* 242–43, 247

Australian bell frogs, *1:* 11

Australian ground frogs, *1:* 124–38, 142

Australian toadlets, *1:* 139–51

Axolotls, *3:* 434

B

Bana leaf litter frogs, *1:* 79, 82–83, 82 (ill.), 83 (ill.)

Banana frogs. *See* Golden treefrogs

Banded rubber frogs, *3:* 387–88, 387 (ill.), 388 (ill.)

Barbourula busuangensis. See Philippine barbourulas

Barbourulas, *1:* 25–43

Baw Baw frogs, *1:* 125, 127–28

Beddome's Indian frogs, *2:* 287

Bell's salamanders, *3:* 491–92, 491 (ill.), 492 (ill.)

Bereis' treefrogs. *See* Hourglass treefrogs

Betic midwife toads, *1:* 48

Betsileo golden frogs, *3:* 350

Betsileo reed frogs, *3:* 334

Bidder's organ, *1:* 2, *2:* 191, 198

Big-eared forest treefrogs, *3:* 333, 335–36

Black eels. *See* Cayenne caecilians

Black-eyed frogs, *2:* 261–62

Bloody Bay poison frogs, *2:* 224

Blue-back frogs. *See* Madagascar reed frogs

Blue-bellied poison frogs, *2:* 220, 222–23

Blue-toed rocket frogs, *2:* 222–23, 232–34, 232 (ill.), 233 (ill.)

Bolitoglossa pesrubra. See Talamancan web-footed salamanders

Bolivian bleating frogs, *3:* 370, 373–74

Bombina bombina. See Fire-bellied toads

Bombina orientalis. See Oriental fire-bellied toads

Bombina variegata. See Yellow-bellied toads

Bombinatoridae. *See* Barbourulas; Fire-bellied toads

Bornean flat-headed frogs, *1:* 29

Borneo tree-hole frogs, *3:* 372

Boulenger's callulops frogs, *3:* 369, 371, 372

Boulenger's climbing frogs, *3:* 372–74

Brachycephalidae. *See* Three-toed toadlets

Brachycephalus. See Three-toed toadlets

Brachycephalus didactyla, 2: 192

Brachycephalus ephippium. See Pumpkin toadlets

Brachycephalus nodoterga, 2: 192–93

Brachycephalus pernix, 2: 192–93

Brachycephalus vertebralis, 2: 192–93

Brachytarsophrys intermedia. See Annam broad-headed toads

Brazil nut poison frogs, *2:* 218–19

Brazilian poison frogs, *2:* 220, 221, 222–23

Brazillian two-toed toadlets, *1:* 1

Breviceps species. *See* Rain frogs

Broad-headed frogs, *1:* 78, *3:* 371

Broad-headed toads, *1:* 79

Brown frogs, *2:* 306–8, 306 (ill.), 307 (ill.)

Brown rain frogs, *3:* 391–92

Brown tree toads, *2:* 200

Bubble frogs. *See* Malaysian painted frogs

Bubbling kassinas, *3:* 334, 339–41, 339 (ill.), 340 (ill.)

Budgett's frogs, *2:* 155, 161–63, 161 (ill.), 162 (ill.)

Buerger's frogs, *3:* 350, 351, 353–54

Bufo marinus. See Marine toads

Bufo periglenes. See Golden toads

Bufonidae. *See* Harlequin frogs; True toads

Bullfrogs, *1:* 3, *2:* 290, 292, 303–5, 303 (ill.), 304 (ill.)

Buried-eyed caecilians, *3:* 522–26

Burmese bubble-nest frogs, *3:* 352

Burmese spadefoot toads, *1:* 78

Burrowing frogs, *3:* 371

Bush squeakers, *2:* 311, 313–14

Bushveld rain frogs, *3:* 369, 370–73

Busuanga jungle toads. *See* Philippine barbourulas

C

Caecilians, *3:* 501–5
    American tailed, *3:* 506–10
    Asian tailed, *3:* 511–16
    buried-eyed, *3:* 522–26
    tailless, *3:* 527–35

Caeciliidae. *See* Tailless caecilians

California giant salamanders, *3:* 427

Discoglossidae. *See* Midwife toads; Painted frogs

Discoglossus pictus. See Painted frogs

Ditch eels. *See* Amphiumas

Dune squeakers. *See* Common squeakers

Dusky gopher frogs, 2: 292

Dusky salamanders, 3: 479–81, 479 (ill.), 480 (ill.)

Dwarf clawed frogs, 1: 64

Dwarf litter frogs, 1: 77

Dwarf sirens, 3: 403–8

E

Eastern gray treefrogs, 2: 262, 3: 351

Eastern narrow-mouthed toads, 3: 378–80, 378 (ill.), 379 (ill.)

Eastern newts, 3: 442

Eastern owl frogs. *See* Giant burrowing frogs

Eastern sign-bearing froglets, 1: 141

Eastern spadefoot toads, 1: 96

Eastern tiger salamanders, 3: 435

Ecuador Cochran frogs, 2: 242–43, 245, 246–47

Ecuadorian marsupial frogs. *See* Riobamba marsupial frogs

Edalorhina perezi. See Perez's snouted frogs

Eggs of frogs, 3: 374

See also specific species

Eiffinger's Asian treefrogs, 3: 351, 352, 353, 355

Endangered species, 1: 4

See also World Conservation Union (IUCN) Red List of Threatened Species; specific species

Environmental effects on frogs and toads, 1: 4, 2: 311

See also specific species

Epicrionops marmoratus. See Marbled caecilians

Epipedobates tricolor. See Phantasmal poison frogs

Ethiopian snout-burrowers, 2: 324

Eungella day frogs. *See* Eungella torrent frogs

Eungella torrent frogs, 1: 140, 148–50, 148 (ill.), 149 (ill.)

European common frogs. *See* Brown frogs

European fire-bellied toads. *See* Fire-bellied toads

European fire salamanders, 3: 450–52, 450 (ill.), 451 (ill.)

European salamanders, 3: 440–60

Eurycea bislineata. See Two-lined salamanders

Eurycea rathbuni. See Texas blind salamanders

F

Fire-bellied toads, 1: 25–43, 30 (ill.), 31 (ill.)

Fire salamanders, 3: 443

Fish and Wildlife Service (U.S.)

on mole salamanders, 3: 435

on salamander and newts, 3: 402

on torrent salamanders, 3: 478, 490

on true frogs, 2: 292

on true toads, 2: 204

Fleay's barred frogs, 1: 128

Fleischmann's glass frogs, 2: 243, 244, 246–48

Fletcher's frogs, 1: 124

Floating spotted frogs. *See* Pointed-tongue floating frogs

Floodplain toadlets, 1: 141

Flying frogs, 3: 350, 352

Foam nest frogs. *See* Gray treefrogs

Folohy golden frogs. *See* Arboreal mantellas

Forest bright-eyed frogs, 3: 351, 354

Forest green treefrogs. *See* Kinugasa flying frogs

Fossil frogs, 1: 10

Free Madagascar frogs, 3: 351–52, 364–66, 364 (ill.), 365 (ill.)

Frog eggs, 3: 374

See also specific species

Frogs, 1: 1–7

African treefrogs, 3: 331–49

Amero-Australian treefrogs, 2: 259–86

Asian toadfrogs, 1: 77–93

Asian treefrogs, 3: 350–67

Australian ground, 1: 124–38, 142

Australian toadlets, 1: 139–51

barbourulas, 1: 25–43

cricket, 2: 310–22

ghost, 1: 110–16

glass, 2: 242–58

harlequin, 2: 198–217, 208 (ill.), 209 (ill.)

leptodactylid, 2: 153–81

Madagascaran toadlets, 3: 390–97

narrow-mouthed, 3: 368–89

New Zealand, 1: 8–16, 18

painted, 1: 44–55, 53 (ill.), 54 (ill.), 132–34, 132 (ill.), 133 (ill.)

parsley, 1: 102–8, 106 (ill.), 107 (ill.)

poison, 2: 218–35

Ruthven's, 2: 236–41, 238 (ill.), 239 (ill.)

Seychelles, 1: 117–23, 121 (ill.), 122 (ill.)

shovel-nosed, 2: 323–29

in space, 1: 63

squeakers, 2: 310–22

Malaysian painted frogs, *3:* 369, 374, 381–83, 381 (ill.), 382 (ill.)

Malcolm's Ethiopian toads, *2:* 202

Mallorcan midwife toads, *1:* 45, 46–48, 49

Manaus slender-legged treefrogs, *2:* 262–63

Mandarin salamanders, *3:* 453–55, 453 (ill.), 454 (ill.)

Mantellas, *3:* 351, 352–53

Mantidactylus liber. See Free Madagascar frogs

Marbled caecilians, *3:* 508–9, 508 (ill.), 509 (ill.)

Marbled shovel-nosed frogs. *See* Marbled snout-burrowers

Marbled snout-burrowers, *2:* 323–24, 325, 327 (ill.)

Marine toads, *2:* 199, 211–13, 211 (ill.), 212 (ill.)

Marsupial frogs. *See* Hip pocket frogs

Masiliwa snout-burrowers, *2:* 326

Mating calls of frogs and toads. *See* Vocalization, in frogs and toads

Maud Island frogs, *1:* 10, 11, 14–16, 14 (ill.), 15 (ill.)

Megophryidae. *See* Asian toadfrogs

Megophrys montana. See Asian horned frogs

Mesoamerican burrowing toads, *1:* **56–61,** 59 (ill.), 60 (ill.)

Mexican burrowing toads. *See* Mesoamerican burrowing toads

Mexican caecilians, *3:* 530–32, 530 (ill.), 531 (ill.)

Micrixalus phyllophilus. See Nilgiri tropical frogs

Micro frogs, *2:* 293–95, 293 (ill.), 294 (ill.)

Microbatrachella capensis. See Micro frogs

Microhylidae. *See* Narrow-mouthed frogs

Midwife toads, *1:* **44–55,** 50 (ill.), 51 (ill.)

Mimicry, *2:* 219–20
    See also Defense mechanisms; specific species

Mississippi gopher frogs. *See* Dusky gopher frogs

Mocquard's rain frogs, *3:* 390–91, 393, 395–97, 395 (ill.), 396 (ill.)

Mole salamanders, *3:* **433–39**

Morelets treefrogs, *2:* 264

Moss frogs, *1:* 141–42

Mottled burrowing frogs. *See* Marbled snout-burrowers

Mottled shovel-nosed frogs. *See* Marbled snout-burrowers

Mount Glorious day frogs, *1:* 143

Mount Glorious torrent frogs. *See* Mount Glorious day frogs

Mountain alligators. *See* Hellbenders

Mountain frogs, *1:* 128

Mountain short-legged toads. *See* Slender mud frogs

Mountain yellow-legged frogs, *2:* 292

Moustache toads, *1:* 77

Mud devils. *See* Hellbenders

Mud-divers. *See* Parsley frogs

Mudpuppies, *3:* **461–70,** 467 (ill.), 468 (ill.)

Müller's plantannas, *1:* 62

Myers' Surinam toads, *1:* 65, 66

Myobatrachidae. *See* Australian toadlets; Water frogs

Nasikabatrachidae. *See* *Nasikabatrachus sahyadrensis*

Nasikabatrachus sahyadrensis, 1: 118, 119

Natal ghost frogs, *1:* 110–11, 112, 114–16, 114 (ill.), 115 (ill.)

Necturus maculosus. See Mudpuppies

Neobatrachus pictus. See Painted frogs

New Guinea bush frogs, *3:* 368–69, 370

New Mexico spadefoot toads, *1:* 97

New Zealand frogs, *1:* **8–16,** 18

Newts, *3:* **398–402, 440–60**

Nicaragua glass frogs, *2:* 242, 243, 244, 245, 246–47

Nigriventer species. *See* Hula painted frogs

Nilgiri tropical frogs, *2:* 299–300, 299 (ill.), 300 (ill.)

Northern banjo frogs, *1:* 124

Northern cricket frogs, *2:* 261, 262

Northern gastric brooding frogs, *1:* 143

Northern spadefoot toads, *1:* 135–37, 135 (ill.), 136 (ill.)

Northern toadlets, *1:* 139

Notaden melanoscaphus. See Northern spadefoot toads

Nsoung long-fingered frogs, *2:* 312, 314

Nuptial pads, *1:* 20
    See also specific species

Nyctixalus pictus. See Painted Indonesian treefrogs

Smooth toadlets, *1:* 141

Sooglossidae. *See* Seychelles frogs

Sooglossus sechellensis. See Seychelles frogs

South American bullfrogs, *2:* 155, 170–72, 170 (ill.), 171 (ill.)

Southern day frogs. *See* Mount Glorious day frogs

Southern gastric brooding frogs, *1:* 143

Southern three-toed toadlets, *2:* 190

Southwestern toads. *See* Arroyo toads

Space, frogs in, *1:* 63

Spadefoot toads, *1:* 94–101

Spea bombifrons. See Plains spadefoot toads

Species
  endangered, *1:* 4
  introduced, *1:* 4, 48–49, *2:* 157
  super, *3:* 336
  See also specific species

Spencer's burrowing frogs, *1:* 124, 126

Sphagnum frogs, *1:* 128

Spiny-headed treefrogs, *2:* 262, 263

Spiny-knee leaf frogs, *2:* 264

Spiny leaf-folding frogs. *See* Greater leaf-folding frogs

Spiracles, *1:* 57

Spix's saddleback toads. *See* Pumpkin toadlets

Splendid poison frogs, *2:* 225

Spotted lazy toads, *1:* 80

Spotted marsh frogs, *1:* 127

Spotted snout-burrowers, *2:* 323–24, 326

Spring lizards. *See* Salamanders

Spring peeper frogs, *1:* 4

Squeakers, *2:* 310–22

Stephen's rocket frogs, *2:* 219, 222

Stonemason toadlets, *1:* 140

Strawberry poison frogs, *2:* 218–19, 221–24

Sumaco horned treefrogs, *2:* 261, 268–70, 268 (ill.), 269 (ill.)

Sunset frogs, *1:* 139

Super species, *3:* 336

Surinam horned frogs, *2:* 155, 158–60, 158 (ill.), 159 (ill.)

Surinam toads, *1:* 62–76, 73–75, 73 (ill.), 74 (ill.)

T

Table Mountain ghost frogs. *See* Rose's ghost frogs

Tadpoles, *1:* 2, 4–5, 57
  See also specific species

Tailed frogs, *1:* 17–24

Tailless caecilians, *3:* 527–35

Talamancan web-footed salamanders, *3:* 484–85, 484 (ill.), 485 (ill.)

Tanner's litter frogs, *2:* 311, 312, 313

Tarantulas and frogs, *3:* 373

Taudactylus eungellensis. See Eungella torrent frogs

Texas blind salamanders, *3:* 489–90, 489 (ill.), 490 (ill.)

Thomasset's frogs, *1:* 117–19

Thoropa miliaris. See Rock river frogs

Three-toed amphiumas, *3:* 498–99, 498 (ill.), 499 (ill.)

Three-toed toadlets, *2:* 190–97

Thumbed ghost frogs. *See* Rose's ghost frogs

Tibetan stream salamanders, *3:* 410

Tiger salamanders, *3:* 436–38, 436 (ill.), 437 (ill.)

Timbo disc frogs, *3:* 373

Tinkling frogs, *1:* 141

Toad-like treefrogs, *3:* 333, 334

Toadlets
  Australian, *1:* 139–51

Madagascaran, *3:* 390–97
  three-toed, *2:* 190–97

Toads, *1:* 1–7
  fire-bellied, *1:* 25–43, 30 (ill.), 31 (ill.)
  Mesoamerican burrowing, *1:* 56–61, 59 (ill.), 60 (ill.)
  midwife, *1:* 44–55, 50 (ill.), 51 (ill.)
  spadefoot, *1:* 94–101
  Surinam, *1:* 62–76, 73–75, 73 (ill.), 74 (ill.)
  true, *2:* 198–217

Tomato frogs, *3:* 371

Torrent salamanders, *3:* 471–75

Transparent reed frogs, *3:* 332

Treefrogs
  African, *3:* 331–49
  Amero-Australian, *2:* 259–86
  Asian, *3:* 350–67

Trichobatrachus robustus. See Hairy frogs

Trilling frogs. *See* Painted frogs

Trinidad poison frogs, *2:* 222, 223

Triprion petasatus. See Yucatecan shovel-headed treefrogs

Triturus cristatus. See Great crested newts

Triturus vulgaris. See Smooth newts

Tropical clawed frogs, *1:* 70–72, 70 (ill.), 71 (ill.)

True frogs, *2:* 287–309, 325

True toads, *2:* 198–217

Túngara frogs, *2:* 156

Turtle frogs, *1:* 139, 140

Tusked frogs, *1:* 129–31, 129 (ill.), 130 (ill.)

Two-lined salamanders, *3:* 486–88, 486 (ill.), 487 (ill.)

Tylototriton verrucosus. See Mandarin salamanders

X

Xenopus laevis. See Common plantannas

Y

Yellow-bellied toads, *1:* 37–40, 37 (ill.), 38 (ill.)

Yellow-legged kassinas, *3:* 332
Yellow-legged treefrogs. *See* Yellow-legged kassinas
Yellow-striped reed frogs, *3:* 332
Yucatecan shovel-headed treefrogs, *2:* 276–77, 276 (ill.), 277 (ill.)

Yungas redbelly toads, *2:* 199, 200, 201
Yunnan moustache toads. *See* Ailao moustache toads

Z

Zimmermann's poison frogs, *2:* 219